C0-ASY-102

Contents

For more than two centuries there has been general agreement that our schools are the cornerstone for the development of citizens and practices for our democracy. Yet, we are stunned by the absence of democratic practices in today's schools. Wouldn't it be curious if, having recognized the importance of math to the development of society, we failed to teach mathematics in our schools? A parallel absurdity confronts us every day through the windows of undemocratic classrooms, schools, and districts.

We are in need of another Grand Experiment. EdVisions Schools are both the grand experiment and the current reality. The Minnesota-based EdVisions Cooperative charter schools aim to establish teacher-led democratic schools. Newell and Buchen firmly believe and argue that lasting change cannot occur within the current structure. By proposing new leadership structures; new partnerships among principals, teachers, and students; and the emergence of teachers as leaders, EdVisions positions its schools on the leading edge of the future.

Constructing the future takes many and congruent paths in EdVisions Schools. Democracy, as well as learning and leading, are constructivist processes as they engage multiple voices, beliefs, and perspectives in the development and critiquing of competing ideas that move us toward consensus and action. This process is often awkward and difficult, and it is also the theater in which we become more fully capable of taking the journey.

In schools, democratic experiences can be established for students as well as adults through choice and voice, involvement in classroom and broader communities, governance, and project-based learning. When we assume that knowledge comes from multiple sources and is mined by self-focused discovery, reflection, and assessment, democracy becomes more than a theory, more than an historical promise. Students and adults become fiercely entrepreneurial and fiercely collaborative as well. A contradiction in terms? I don't think so. Newell and Buchen envision that such complex democratic schools can grow from the EdVisions principles of democracy, equity, clarity of value and roles, comparable worth, quality, and competency.

Teacher leadership efforts, while growing tremendously in this country, have been like swimming uphill. Numerous universities now offer degrees in teacher leadership, yet these leaders often live out their professional lives in traditional, hierarchical schools. Many schools are nurturing and expanding teacher leadership only to be restricted by districts in which policies for resource distribution, evaluation, tenure, and accountability limit its possibilities. Does it have to be so difficult? Why can't we just design schools as teacher-led, democratic places?

The authors are not naïve enough to think that teachers, by their very nature, are more inherently democratic than others. We share the belief that leading and democratic practice is skillful and learnable work. I have long assumed that each person has the right, responsibility, and capability to be a leader. Two particular challenges present themselves: we must define leadership with enough breadth that teachers can realize that this is their work, and teachers need to hone their own identities to make room for leadership. Defining leadership as purposeful learning in community invites teachers to move toward the interaction of three intricately interconnected actions: learning, teaching, and leading.

In this forthrightly honest and thoughtful book, the founders of the EdVisions Cooperative are modeling the transparency about which they speak. They reveal their warts as well as their gems by evaluating themselves and looking hard at the feedback provided by participants. If there were not struggles, I would not find this effort as credible. The struggles are not unfamiliar to all schools: time, conflicting priorities, the need for democratic skills for working together, the difficulty of implementing peer coaching, as well as dominant behaviors and reticent personalities who draw back from declaring themselves to be leaders. If these struggles are so familiar to us, how is this effort different?

This effort is different because participants also report that being an engaged member of a democratic school has provided:

- A more cohesive and integrated sense of purpose, goals, and measurements for success;
- A greater sense of involvement in and responsibility for the school program;
- A means for providing more attention to students and parents;
- A greater sense of involvement and responsibility for students.

These findings persuade me to believe that the philosophy, structures, and opportunities in place are providing the context within which the inhabitants of these schools will tackle and resolve the challenges that they encounter.

Organization patterns for shared governance and accountability create the conditions within which the work of these schools unfold. Opportunities for democratic governance and for learning these practices exist in thoughtful roles for teachers—framed by a Collaborative Spectrum that defines the breadth of tasks within a "traditional," "transitional," and "transformational" continuum, that reflects an understanding that this work is developmental rather than a series of events. The Five Facets of Collaboration plumb the depths of professional practice in schools from collective work to creating community. Both vertical and lateral frames create a learning and leading culture.

I would be delighted if this book described most schools. It does not. We are in dire need of experiencing and understanding schools as they might be. Schools have been in a responding mode for too long—responding to external mandates, power moves, political pressures, and resource manipulation. Schools can lead rather than respond. They can lead us toward a desired future for both education and society. Newell and Buchen let us look through that window of possibility into a future in which schools can lead democratic change in our country because they are vibrant laboratories for this essential work.

Linda Lambert

Introduction

The emergence of a new education culture of democratic collaborative participation has taken two forms. The first is gradual and evolutionary. It involves a rapprochement of supervisors and teachers. Although the arrangements may vary, greater equity is a constant. The other is more radical and discontinuous. It involves teachers stepping forth as leaders in their own right without becoming principals but still remaining in the classroom as teachers. It is burdened with the task of creating both a new collaborative culture and a democratized governance structure, and ideally fusing the two.

The first step was principal and teacher partnerships that began the culture of leadership sharing. Site-based management mandated in the 1970s established a degree of consultation between educational constituencies that could not be reversed. Indeed, an increasing number of principals took the initiative subsequently to form or expand governance relationships with teachers. Predictably, it ranged from a still-tight administrative control at one extreme to near-total equity at the other.

Often, such initiatives were criticized by other principals in the same district; and when that enterprising administrator left or was replaced, the structure of consultation often was abandoned. Nevertheless, progress continued. Indeed, that was given a strong boost by the recent call for principals to play a greater role as instructional leaders. Although that involved many areas, clearly a central element involved greater cooperation and involvement by teachers; and so the movement toward teacher governance was thereby reinforced.

The net result is the end of the principal as the lone leader. What has emerged, admittedly more as a promise than as a pattern, is the structure of shared leadership. To many principals that is anathema. They would rather quit than share. Others, especially those newly entering administration, have a more open mind and want to know more about the options. They want to know what authority they have to give up or share, and what the research shows as to the impact of the linkage between governance and teacher performance and its effect on student achievement.

In short, there is no clear-cut evidence that leadership sharing will become a dominant pattern. Right now it is more the exception than the rule. It is more a metaphor of what should be than what is. Although for many schools it is a next step contemplated but not generally taken, its gains are real and substantial.

But for many teachers, such straddling fell short of meeting their objections and matching their aspirations. The next step of partnership did not go far enough. It still was too dependent on the largesse of principals. And they in turn were ruled by superintendents and school boards. Teachers did not consistently select curricula. And even when they did, the district often selected the texts. Above all, access to decision making was often partial and limited. It did not really offer democracy.

In short, it had all the characteristics of a compromise; for some teachers that was not good enough. They valued the special leadership teachers alone could provide but did not wish to be forced to leave the classroom and become administrators. The teachers wished in fact to position the classroom and curricula as the central focus of administration and thus have the entire enterprise managed as it were from within, always by insiders. They also wanted to explore creating a general structure of school management that would be so democratic that it would include and be shaped by all its constituents: teachers, parents, students, and board members. Above all, they wanted to bring together professional conversations and systemic planning, and thereby align learning objectives with school and community objectives. Thus emerged the teacher as leader and a culture interdependently collaborative and democratic.

Of course, the obstacles were enormous. Initially and even subsequently it was an ad hoc world. Everything was created daily on the fly. What was put together one day often had to be revised the next day. Everything was fluid. Transition became not only a norm but also a permanent condition. Just surviving and managing the turbulence was sufficient. Type As would never be able to do either. At the end of every week, the structure of putting Humpty Dumpty back together again and again was viewed. Whatever pride was expressed was matched by the conclusion that we are not there yet. At times it appeared nothing would ever achieve final status because the scaffolding was constantly being redesigned.

Other difficulties were psychological and cultural, self-defining and structural. First, no one is currently being trained in colleges of education as teacher leaders. Educational leadership is reserved for administrators. Second, most teachers reflect the values the national culture puts on rugged individualism and pulling oneself by one's own bootstraps—hence, teacher independence—and the respect Americans are to show to their elders and authority in general—hence dependence. Third, teaching does not generally attract and retain renegades, reformers, or ambitious types. Ambitious ones have only one way to go: leaving the classroom and becoming an administrator. Fourth, most teachers believe that their plate is already too full, especially when considering what they are paid. Why take on more, and more that is unknown, for the same salary? Finally, bewilderment and skepticism appeared. Is teacher leadership another flavor of the month—a new flash in the pan—that may not last or offer any security? Besides, if one concludes that if it is tried and found not your cup of tea, where do you go from there? On the basis of the discussion here, it would appear that there would be no takers. But there are—a small minority, accompanied by a larger group looking it over to see if they should take the plunge.

Who are these teacher leaders? They range from new inexperienced teacher graduates, to mature and seasoned teachers with twenty or more years of teaching experience, to some former principals who wanted to go back to working with students, to some retired teachers who wanted to get back in harness in a different way. Generally, they have no administrative ambitions, and their commitment to teaching is absolute. They usually find it especially attractive to being involved in curricula options such as project or service learning that require a high degree of student involvement and decision making.

Above all, the experienced teachers have concluded that no real or lasting change in education is possible given its generally systemic inflexibility and top-down administrative control. They are tired of not being listened to or when asked being ignored. They believe they are as smart as the best administrators and know what it takes to set up and run a school. And they know what is required to create and sustain a structure which accommodates and optimizes teacher leadership and a learning community.

It is with this optimistic view we undertake to describe what is happening in a very particular set of circumstances: the movement of educators attempting to establish schools inherently democratic, both for students in their learning program and also in management of schools. These schools are part of EdVisions Schools, an organization funded by the Bill and Melinda Gates Foundation that creates and sustains small, project-based, democratic schools and asks that teachers manage the whole of the school business. At the point of this writing, twelve new schools have been created, most with a democratic management led by the teachers, with no designated principals or superintendents. What is presented here is a work in progress. We are learning something new with each school. What we know now is that the work must be intentional, that new forms of school cultures have to be cultivated, and that they depend on both the past and the future vision.

CHAPTER 1

The Future of School Governance

That which is creative must create itself.

—John Keats

Strange as it may seem, the future exists in three different forms: past driven, present driven, and future driven. That mixture has always existed with generally the same proportions of one-third each. But distortions of the normal distribution sometimes occur. When they do, presumptive or obscurative factors, or a blend of both, minimize the future.

The past can become so urgent, powerful, and tenacious that it arrogantly displaces or empties the future of its unique content. Or the momentum of continuity is so reassuring that it appears to hide or trivialize new developments. In education, past-driven futures appear in the efforts of the professional associations of both educational administrators and of teachers to preserve their traditional roles, especially leadership roles. Administrators lead, teachers follow; principals supervise, teachers teach. The gap is the gap, and that is that. They are never part of the same professional association. They never meet together in conferences.

Currently two specific, past-oriented urgencies respectively are being pushed forward. Principals are being urged by their professional associations to become instructional leaders (which must come as a surprise to many who have been doing that for years). Unions are pushing for teachers to have more control over curriculum (which already prevails in many school districts). In both instances, the emphasis is obviously not so much on what is being sought or fought, since that is already in hand, but on achieving political positioning to lay claim to a piece of the future.

The present is no less dispossessing of the future. It is dominated by heavyweights with strong national leverage. There is the megaforce of No Child Left Behind, the pressure of legislatures and school boards for accountability, a bewildering array of positive and negative reward and punishment incentive systems, and the backlash of zero tolerance. Never before have so many imposing, invasive, and external forces taken over education. Virtually all the traditional constituencies of administrators, teachers, parents, and students are dwarfed by these colossi striding across education. The net result is that the future of the future may already have been compromised.

However, what we modestly would like to suggest is that education has been reinventing itself by developing new and different educational leaders. And what is striking about this new leadership is that it is shared across the aisle by both principals and teachers. It has not just happened, nor is it a pipe dream of years to come. It already enjoys a reasonably long and respectable past, a strong and stirring present, and if we only clear enough space in front of us in the future for something genuinely new and transforming to emerge, educational leadership may be one of the most significant agents of school reform.

Although only the highlights are presented here, in a nutshell what we are describing is a convergence of three developments: the appearance of new leadership governance structures, new partnerships between principals and teachers, and the separate emergence of teachers as leaders and even owners. Individually and collectively, they embody a series of quiet but major leadership role changes ranging from the moderate to the radical. Although these have not generally been acknowledged, they may become the means by which educators—all of them—may not only provide education with its future direction but also reposition educators from the periphery to the center. Allow us to sketch the case in limited terms to at least justify our rhetorical hope.

In the last two decades, a wonderfully complicated patchwork of developments has appeared. Not surprisingly, they are the creations of flexible and experimental principals and of strong and assertive teachers. In the process, leadership gradually abandoned its monolithic character and exhibited the spread of a spectrum. It ran from totally dominant principals at one end to teachers as principals at the other. In between were a number of variations on a unique arrangement of leadership sharing. As initially unofficial and unsanctioned new governance arrangements emerged to bridge gaps, leadership roles began to change for both principals and teachers. Although it took many forms, the following six basic patterns facilitated and structured those role changes: site-based management, principal–teacher partnerships, leadership and learning school councils, distributed leadership, teacher leadership, and teacher ownership.

1. *Site-based management:* This coalition of teachers with principals still presiding was less the result of democratic governance than it was the pressure for greater decentralization. Not accidentally, it emerged at a time when individual schools were acquiring local community school boards and when the differences of school demographics were dramatically apparent. But whatever the initial impetus, site-based management became the unofficial training ground of leadership development for teachers. The process also planted the seeds of later teacher leadership recognition and experimentation by both principals and teachers. Indeed, the current successful experiment in New York City of decentralized budgeting based on performance and localized in each school derives from and extends principles of site-based management.

2. *Principal–teacher partnerships*: Where site-based management did not exist or where its range was limited, a number of principals took the initiative of forming governance partnerships (Sergiovanni 1994). Although it remained basically a recommending body with the principal still making the final decisions, it considerably enlarged the leadership range of teachers, provided more access of instruction to administration, and delivered more cooperative coherence to school operations. But generally it would not have happened without the experimentation of some bold principals. Proof of that is twofold: often they were criticized by other principals in the school district; and when they left, top-down ways of doing things returned.

3. *Leadership and learning school councils*: Once again, principals are the key. The principal of McCosh Elementary School in Chicago is typical. These councils pushed the envelope further in at least three ways. First, learning and leadership were fused. The classroom was the direct focus of administration. Second, the council ran the school. Directives were issued and signed by the council. Third, the role of the principal became that of steward. He or she made the council aware of the political waters that had to be navigated and where policy and budgetary adjustments had to be made. The principal remained the school's advocate and carried forward and argued for the acceptance of the proposals. Although in many cases what these councils recommended was often no different from those of other schools, the difference mainly resided in the speed and harmony of implementation.

4. *Distributed leadership*: This contribution especially urged by Richard Elmore (1996) argued that administrators should not enjoy a monopoly on leadership. It should available to all. Written into each employee's job description, teachers should be free to exercise leadership within their own spheres of operation. The net result is that leadership is not held tight but shared, not restricted but distributed. Elmore urged further that principals, hopefully through governance forums, develop the general parameters of leadership options. That once set in place, teachers individually can make decisions about their classrooms on their own. The net effect would be system of independent and often autonomously distributed or minileadership options that extended and supplemented those of the principal.

5. *Teacher leadership*: Up to this point, the process of role change has been incremental. Teachers exercised more leadership; administrators were involved in more flexible sharing arrangements. But the variables in the equation still remained teachers and principals. With the emergence of teacher leadership, that changes radically. What appears is the teacher as principal. Although that role has been ideologically explored by many (Barth, Young, et al.), it remained essentially an aspirational metaphor. It certainly was never put forward as substitutive. No one went the

next step and envisioned teachers sans principals. What hastened its happening were five factors.

The first, sadly, is not new. It derives from the generally unhappy experience of many teachers with administrators, especially through the evaluation process. Increasingly, teachers believed that the price of having someone in the front office to take the heat was too high. The indispensability of principals, based on their performance and often autocratic ways, was being questioned.

The second was the prospect of new structural designs. Charter schools provided a blank slate. Typically, the start-up group consisted only of teachers or a combination of teachers and ex-administrators. Most were mature and seasoned. Many had cut their leadership teeth on various governance structures and affirmed the power and intelligence of collaborative decision making. They were not cocky, but they were confident that they could run schools if that role was built in from the start.

The third factor was economic. Designers of new charter schools, realizing they had limited allocated funds per capita to work with and recognizing that they had to remain solvent, reviewed where they could save. The costs associated with administration were too substantial and tempting to ignore. Whether economics or ideology determined the acceptance by teachers of the ultimate leadership role is a chicken-and-egg problem. But, clearly, cost savings drove teachers to be principals and accordingly to further embrace distributed leadership.

The fourth factor involved taking a leaf from the business research. Christensen (2000) and others had found that wherever organizations spawned new offshoots, those that were obediently imitative and also remained tightly part of the original company either failed or did poorly. But those that were free to create their own organic system prospered. Many charter school designers and consultants were aware of the need to strike out in new directions; others favored the tried and true.

Finally, there was the unique challenge of eliminating or closing the traditional gap between teachers and administration. The goal for the first time would be a total integration of administration, instruction, and evaluation. Decisions would not have to be piecemeal or handled sequentially by different and often conflicting perspectives. Seamlessly, the administrative, instructional, and evaluative dimensions could all be inclusively and holistically factored together. Classroom and student performance remained the center. Everything functional and contributory to that focus formed a ring around it. Only a small number of charter schools elected this unique direction. But their success created real models to observe and emulate and above all to demonstrate the efficacy of teacher leadership.

6. *Teacher ownership*: In many ways this is icing on the cake. It adds to and intensifies teacher leadership to the point where it actually involves ownership. As described by Dirkswager's (2002) *Teachers as Owners*, ownership is not merely a symbolic claim but an actual fact. Ownership recovers professionalism. As owners, teachers can contract and negotiate with clients the terms of their service. They are direct agents of their own professionalism. They are not the employees of school boards or districts. They are their own agents in a competitive marketplace. As a cooperative, they share all the risks and the benefits of the operation, and governance is totally collaborative.

What conclusions, no matter how tentative, can be drawn at this point? The first and most obvious is the recognition that leadership is not singular but multiple and that it now inhabits a spectrum. All six versions coexist. The traditional situation of the solitary and strong principal is no longer the dominant mode. Second, little or no change would have occurred without the initiative of many bold principals who often risked much in opening the floodgates. To be sure, some were nudged or coaxed by equally adventuresome teachers. Adversarial relationships that ensure the status quo were replaced by leadership sharing. Third, of all the various role changes, the last two are out of the box, including Pandora's. They break away from the incremental pattern and strike out in a totally new direction. This new direction is the riskiest of all. At this point it is primarily tied to the fledgling charter movement, and at best it is a small minority effort in terms of numbers. Yet in spite or because of that, it is stirring. Fourth, leadership sharing has led to a more shared concentrated focus on learning; to the greater integration of administration, instruction, and evaluation; and finally to the emergence of collaborative governance structures.

Who is running the future? The new educational leaders, that's who. Putting educators back in charge of education requires a vision of collaborative leadership between principals and teachers, or teachers and teachers. Leadership sharing may be a future whose time has come.

In the following pages are stories and cases of real teachers who are sharing leadership, even ownership, of the educational enterprise; a position in which teachers have had very little practice. There are perils and problems in attempting a newly devised model. There are also promises in this form of collaboration that may revitalize education. But we need to recognize that the culture of teaching has a number of obstacles and roadblocks that keep teachers from attaining democratic, collaborative governance.

CHAPTER 2

The Teacher Culture of the Past and Present

There is a special art to reading the recommendations of national commission reports. It involves not only the familiar practice of reading between the lines but also perceiving the negatives that lurk behind the recommendations as well as what may prevent them from being sustained later on. Here, then, is a blow-by-blow translation of the not-so-hidden agenda and assumptions behind the recommendation:

Teachers are generally not empowered.

Teachers typically do not have control, creative or otherwise, over curriculum.

If and when control is granted, teachers have to accept responsibility for student performance.

Committees are not normally forms of governance.

Rather, committees of teachers are essentially operational and administrative in nature.

Teachers are limited to making recommendations that the principal may or may not accept.

Often teachers are not asked to assist at all.

Seldom if ever do teachers coordinate schoolwide programs.

The domino theory prevails: often even the principal in turn has limited autonomy.

Local or site-based decision making is often constrained by policy and checked by multiple layers of external approval.

No wonder a recommendation was needed! There is so much that is not going on, and so little coherence with what is, that it would be more accurate to sum up the situation of many teachers as a series of gaps. Like the emperor who wears no clothes, the issues remain unaddressed. Even national reports sometimes use doublespeak to refer indirectly to inequities and gaps wide and frequent enough to let students and much more fall between them. In other words, to understand adequately both the present and future of education, it is necessary to understand the culture of teachers.

The teacher may begin the day before the students arrive in order to do some advanced preparation or use the copy machine before anyone else does or before the paper supply gives out or the machine breaks down. The classroom may have been built decades ago and now has peeling paint and inscribed desks; or it may be more modern and even be equipped with a combo TV/VCR or computer, donated by the parent–teacher organization (PTO). On average a teacher meets five to six classes each day for about an hour each. When not teaching, she catches up on her many clerical tasks. In England, that work is estimated to total 16 percent of a typical work week of fifty-two hours. The only contacts the teacher has with adults are brief and either social or disciplinary. Often she skips lunch and snacks at her desk.

Work done on the curriculum and on examining student work is done in isolation. Department meetings usually are preoccupied with announcing the latest from on high. District administrators usually select the texts each grade level will use.

The structure of the school and the tyranny of time, place, and workload provide little opportunity to reflect individually or with other professionals. The teacher is like a plant manager who also works on the assembly line. She has to plan and produce at the same time. To shift the metaphor, she is like the quarterback who throws the ball and then has to run down field to catch it as well. Then, too, no one teaching the same subject or same grade level really knows what the others are doing. They are all like parallel lines that never meet.

Teachers, new or old, routinely experience benign abandonment. The teacher is on her own. She is left to her own devices to interpret and select classroom techniques. The only feedback she receives is from the annual evaluation of the principal, which may be so partial or petty as to be either useless or an irritant. Occasionally a student or a parent will make her day with praise. Teachers have thin skins, and their egos bruise easily. The more dedicated and original among them seem to suffer more.

The value of understanding the routine and general isolation of teachers is that it constitutes the culture of instruction. As such it serves as a benchmark against which proposed changes can be intelligently evaluated. For example, reducing class size and/or extending the length of the day or of the school year may increase student access to learning, but it does not increase teacher's access to planning or to other teachers. The further problem with such single focused and quantitative solutions is that they provide only partial solutions. They are exclusive, not inclusive. They do not incorporate all the players. The dynamic in this case is one-sided: students, not teachers. What is the value of reducing class size if what actually takes place with fewer students is still the same old questionable stuff decided on in the same unconsultative way? We have improved the scabbard but left untouched the unsharpened sword.

Worse of all when reductions in class size do not work or fail to accomplish all that was initially claimed, the public or parents are either confused or throw up their hands in despair. Nothing seems to work. Look at all the money we throw at the problem. It is hopeless.

But teachers themselves are the problem. They prefer being Lone Rangers. They have a fetish about being totally in charge of their classroom. They relish closing the door of their classroom and, like judges in a courtroom, reigning supreme. But it seems odd that for a profession to be based so totally on communications skills to be reluctant or downright resistant to sharing ideas. In other words, the chosen isolation of teachers cannot be finally understood without understanding their total culture.

The teacher culture is a paradox of being isolated and yet wanting to share. Meritocracy must never be allowed to prevail. No one teacher can be seen as better as or more expert than another. Generally, teachers do not stand up at faculty meetings and declare, "I have a great idea and I want to share it with you." Such a statement breaks the unwritten and unspoken rule that no teacher may be considered more talented or more capable than any other. The teacher culture not only enforces isolation and precludes collaboration but also endorses mediocrity.

Those singled out for praise are usually put down as the principal's pet or public relations experts heavily engaged in self-advertisement. Even those who receive bonuses or incentive pay for increasing test scores are perceived as political animals who, like their students, know how to work the system and to make it pay. Awards, local, regional, or national, do not really bring about change among the core of the teacher corps. Like the top salespeople who every year win the trip to Hawaii, every one already knows in advance who will receive the Golden Apple Award or be subsidized to undertake national certification. In fact, they all often are visibly engaged in a campaign to win recognition. And such a situation generally works, but it seldom if ever changes the teacher culture or alters the mainstream of collective ordinariness and anonymity.

Why and how did that mainstream come about and become dominant? Competition in other professions (e.g., doctors, lawyers, Indian chiefs) seems to work—why not education? Two reasons, perhaps. First, schools are everywhere and labor-intensive. They employ thousands locally and millions nationally. Thus, the bell curve rules. The small percentage of the best is offset by the equal percentage of the worst. The bulk is in the middle. Neither outstanding nor inadequate, they are average. Furthermore, it is the role of unions and of professional associations to protect the average and to argue not unconvincingly that it is good enough to be acceptable. That middle group creates the mainstream of the teacher culture. To preserve its centrality, it must remain intact. It must not invite or suffer any comparison. It must share the hair shirt isolation of its common identity.

Failing to understand the inertia and quiet opposition of the teacher culture leads once again to the development and advocacy of a number of obvious or highly touted solutions that fail because they fall short of engaging underlying realities. For example, a favorite campaign is to raise starting salaries so that they are more competitive or to designate certain teachers as master teachers who will then earn more. But that does not alter the basic mainstream or affect the distribution of the bell curve. It may increase slightly the number of those who are outstanding, but it does not alter the basic numbers or the inward solidarity of the average teacher culture. It is not unlike the distribution of SAT scores. Although many more are taking the exam, the percentage of top scores has changed very little. If education is really to change, the focus must be on the big middle group.

The second reason stems from the strong contribution of the national culture to the teacher culture. Generally teachers are not expected to and hence are not taught to work together. In Japan where the national culture stresses the group rather than the individual, the school day is made longer in large part to facilitate grade-level or subject-matter meetings. Teachers discuss with their colleagues their teaching plans and methodologies. Suggestions are made and often incorporated. Perhaps because it is done privately and in a face-saving manner, teachers can then go forth now armed and amplified with the feedbacks and insights of others and still be perceived as in charge.

Consultation in Asian cultures tends to be not only a norm but also comprehensive. That is the way Japanese corporations, for example, develop their strategic plans. Unlike the American version that hurries forward by minimizing input and often falls apart later, Asian corporations take longer but implement faster because everyone already has had the chance to provide input. A favorite Japanese proverb is "The nail that sticks up gets pounded down."

But national cultures are subject to changing dynamics. In the United States, competition has forced business to change its culture and paradigm of operation. Workers and customers have been invested with greater importance. To increase productivity, employees used to working individually under the all-knowing gaze of supervisors have had to become problem solvers and work in self-managing teams. Indeed, many of the gains in productivity, profitability, and even quality in the last two decades have been the result of these new structures and cultures of cooperation.

Teams do not require the elevation of the superior individual performer but only that of the collective effort. The bell curve still operates but floats at a higher overall level. Thus, although teams vary, the mainstream is notched up by virtue of its collective aspiration and upgrading of its goals. The superior teams set the standards. The poor teams shape up or are dismantled and reassembled.

But the teacher culture faces a double problem. First, the profession itself generally has not been trained to work as a team. Second, the work environment and administration do not encourage or facilitate collective engagement.

Outsiders are often puzzled by the contradictory image of teachers: tigers in the classroom and pussycats at meetings; decisive and clear in parent–teacher conferences, tentative or quiet in public. In November 1993, then–Secretary of Education Richard Riley called a forum of teachers together to discuss the Goals 2000 program. The title of the issued report was "Honor What We Know, Listen to What We Say."

Unlike the recommendation from the Carnegie report that had to be tweaked and teased to get at its hidden meaning, here the title and report says it all: Teachers are smart; teachers know what they are talking about; do not ignore or bypass their knowledge; tap and use it; above all, listen to what they have to say.

The report goes on to describe how in many ways teachers "are not taken seriously. If they were, they would be actively involved in policy making at all levels" (U.S. Department of Education 1993).

Would all teachers agree? Surely, all would concur with the basic premise: that they all know what they are doing and that their knowledge is seldom tapped. But many would step back from wanting to be engaged in political decision making, let alone at all levels. Most would argue that is not what teachers do; that is what principals do. Furthermore, if that is what some teachers want to do, then they should become administrators. That is how some teachers unknowingly devalue the knowledge of their colleagues and in the process establish the limits of their governance.

In the future, such either-or choices may not operate; teachers may not have to leave the classroom to be leaders. But the mind-set of separation persists in most schools and school districts. Principals still rule, and the title of the report remains unheeded.

Sergiovanni (1994) characterizes the leadership style of educational administrators as "Follow Me" leadership. Teachers not unhappily follow this kind of leadership because it has the authority to command obedience in the same trickle-down way they would wish their students to obey and follow them. Then, too, principals are often adept at bribery and fear, distributing goodies or dispensing devaluative looks or memos. Teachers submit to the establishment of a hierarchical form of authority and accept the role of subordinates who must be constantly watched over lest they fail or stray. Not unlike the social parable in Ibsen's *A Doll's House*, it is the father's duty to prepare the subjugation of his daughter when he passes her on to the new authority of her husband. Given the number of women in teaching and the number of men as administrators, gender may play a key role in sustaining father always knows best. Significantly, as feminism took hold and as more principals were women, teachers were less submissive.

But the net effect has been and still is to some extent what Sergiovanni points out: teachers often are not aggressive because they work in a structure that tells them they know nothing or little. In addition, the lack of support for teachers as professionals is reinforced often through in-service programs designed by administrators. A five-year study of sixteen schools by a UCLA team headed up by Jennie Oakes found that most professional development programs were run by expert outsiders, most of whom were not classroom teachers. Much of what they offered was irrelevant to the classroom, and no follow-up or subsequent support was scheduled. Savvy classroom teachers would never do either.

Principals affect teacher response. In a number of cases, that reinforces teacher isolation through divide and conquer and results in the dominance model of influence. To take hold, it requires regular demonstrations of dominance. Of course, motives must never be impugned. For example, a principal concerned about a school board's recent discussion about students' unhappiness with school announces that all teachers have to meet with their students individually in their homerooms to discuss their student's feelings about school. He proudly strides back into his office and sends a note to tell the superintendent about this initiative, copies every member of the school board, and subsequently includes it in his monthly report to parents. Meanwhile, the teachers whose work conditions have been altered without their consent are asked to undertake something that is perhaps questionable. They also conclude that it won't answer the concerns raised by the principal in the first place, shake their heads in familiar bewilderment, and chalk up the experience to another demonstration of dominance.

But the fallout is severe. Cynicism drives withdrawal and withdrawal drives cynicism. Even new teachers quickly learn that real participation and competence are not valued or evaluated, that obedience can be given its superficial due, and that they are playing with a loaded deck that is stacked against them. Perhaps saddest of all is what is lost is teachers' trust and competence. Teachers converse with their colleagues more openly and at a much higher level when they are participating in real decision making, on the one hand; and when they are working with an authentic and nonmanipulative principals, on the other. But the absence of opportunity and the persistence of dominance continues the vicious cycle: not trusting the administration is directly correlated to not trusting other teachers.

Pulling together the discussion of teachers, their culture, and their role in affecting school reform and student performance, the following common obstacles emerge:

The culture of teachers and the structures of their working conditions are often left out of the solutions loop.

Reducing class size or increasing salaries fails to engage the issue of overcoming teacher isolation.

The knowledge of teachers is routinely undervalued and underutilized.

The structure and design of education frustrates or precludes intelligent and collaborative planning and learning exchanges between teachers.

Ultimately, that trickles down and affects the exchanges between teachers and students, between teachers and parents, and between students and students.

Dominating administrators secure token obedience at the expense of quality participation.

In class, teachers generally are independent, sometimes excessively so. In meetings, especially those presided over by the principal, teachers generally are dependent, sometimes excessively so. What is generally lacking is a culture of interdependence. That, in turn, is shaped by two dynamics: relationships and community.

Ideally, schools should be noisy, engaging places. Silence between teachers signals acceptance, even affirmation, of their isolation from each other. Respect for each other's privacy and domain makes a virtue out of independence and turns it into an end rather than a means of respectful exchange between colleagues and partners. Kids do not have to be taught how to take but how to share. Teachers have to do both.

Teachers have to use each other not because they are weak or dumb but because they know how hard it is to be effective in class; they need all the help that fellow professionals can give. Genuine and authentic interdependence is never judgmental. Rather, it is the way a community of best practices is, in fact, shaped by professionals. It is the way they live and work together. Indeed, what teachers gradually recognize is that such a community is not given or prescribed but, in fact, is shaped and created by teachers themselves. Thus, the form it takes is as varied as teachers and schools themselves.

Moreover, coincidental with the emergence of a culture of community is a pedagogical model that inclusively and interactively involves all learning partners: teachers, parents, and students. Inevitably, some teachers take the next step and push that envelope further by seeking direct and comprehensive involvement in decision making and policy formulation. Inevitably, an interdependent community seeks interdependent governance.

As teachers develop closer and more interactive relationships with each other, it is perhaps inevitable that they recognize the extent to which administrative decisions and policies constrain and even determine their teaching options and even their independence. Often they are locked out of definitions of what constitutes student success even though their expertise should clearly be valued. The ability and freedom of teachers to forge a new dynamic of interdependence with each other and their constituencies runs smack into the wall of limited governance and authority.

What intensifies the situation is that the role of teachers has gradually increased over time through empowering governance structures to the point where those greater freedoms cannot be taken back. In fact, the empowerment process and structures contained within them generate an expectation of further or greater spheres of influence. Above all, the pressures of accountability and high-stakes testing have put the spotlight so intensely on teacher performance that teachers are asking for a greater say on what and how they are to be judged. Thus, a new agenda has emerged: finding a form of community that welcomes professional relationships—in short, shaping a culture of interdependent and democratic governance.

CHAPTER 3

The Past Creates the Future: Democratic Schools

Democracy must be incorporated into learning—for oneself, from and with others. Only then will it become an everyday way of life, a way of self-governance, and a way of "walking the talk."

—John Dewey

Carl Glickman (2001) in his book *Revolutionizing America's Schools* says that the American public learns how to be democratic by being educated in a democratic way. The public schools were created to have a place whereby America's youth would learn the rudiments of democracy and, consequently, America would be transformed into a more democratic society. The means by which democracy is learned is by allowing students to *live* democratic ideals, not just *learn about* them. We wholeheartedly agree that schools are a place for the American public to learn the basic concepts and actions of democratic action.

Therefore, public schools, by virtue of being publicly funded for the very reason of maintaining and renewing our democracy, have "a greater responsibility to practice what they preach—in pedagogy, in operations, and in governance" (Glickman 2001:23). Certain conditions ought to be met if a school were to be called a democratic school: students would be actively working with problems, ideas, materials, and people as they learn skills and content; students would have escalating degrees of choices, both as individuals and as groups, within the parameters provided by the teacher; students would be responsible to peers, to teachers, to parents, and to the school community to ensure educational time is being used purposefully and productively; students would share their learning with one another, with teachers, and with parents and other community members; students would decide how to make a contribution to their community; students would assume escalating responsibility for securing resources (of people and materials outside school) and for finding places where they can apply and further their learning; students would demonstrate what they know and can do in public settings and receive public feedback; and students would work and learn from one another, individually and in groups, at a pace that challenges all (Glickman 2001).

Ensuring such conditions are available for schoolchildren is not an easy thing to accomplish. There are few schools in the nation that adhere to all of the principles just described. There are reasons, many of which have been stated in the past chapter. But there is more to democratic schools than allowing choices and community service classes.

Apple and Beane (1995) say that the democratic way of life is made up of the following conditions: the open flow of ideas, regardless of their popularity, that enables people to be as fully informed as possible; the use of critical reflection and analysis to evaluate ideas, problems, and policies; concern for the welfare of others and the "common good"; and the organization of social institutions to promote and extend the democratic way of life. If these principles refer to the whole operation of the school, Glickman and Apple and Beane are in agreement: democracy is a way of life learned by living the very principles that are its components.

Schools ought to be the place where the young are to learn the means by which they are empowered to become members of the democratic public. Students ought to be allowed to participate in decision making, be involved in issues of governance and policymaking, and be involved in committees and councils. Also, it means that students ought to be involved in making choices along with teachers in collaborative planning, curricular matters, and other issues that affect their collective lives. Certainly they ought to be involved in reflection on what they are learning and why they are learning it.

All of these democratic pedagogical practices are rarely carried on in most schools, let alone being the norm. But the aforementioned practices are carried on wholly or partially in most of the schools created by EdVisions Schools. In these schools, students assume a great role in their own education, learning to take responsibility for greater amounts of choices in their learning and in their actions. EdVisions Schools insists that students do projects that get them involved in learning content from interests, authentic situations, people in real-life situations, and investigation of community problems and situations. Students investigate, either individually or in groups; link their learning to state standards; and present their findings to staff, each other, and the community. Also, EdVisions Schools insists on democratic practices within the school, with student voices being heard and students being allowed some decision making within the boundaries of the school.

As Glickman (2001) goes on to say, "Teachers . . . should never disregard their primary responsibilities of helping students gain greater control over their own education and preparing them for a life of learning" (36). This is the mission and vision of EdVisions Schools: to give the students the responsibility to take over their own learning and become life-long learners and become fully participating democratic citizens.

In addition to creating an atmosphere for students to practice the democratic ideals, Glickman and Apple and Beane allude to another important aspect of democratic schools: that of teachers being given greater control over the educational enterprise. Glickman (2001) adds, "A prerequisite for any school wishing to fulfill democratic pedagogical intentions is to create organizational structures that allow for stable, familiar, and purposeful learning communities among teachers and students" (40). The organizational structure includes not only curricular activities but also active and actual governance procedures. According to Glickman, a democratic school "retains its autonomy in planning, decision-making, hiring, purchasing, and budgeting" (41). Apple and Beane (1995) concur. "Democratic schools are meant to be democratic places, so the idea of democracy also extends to the many roles that adults play in schools. This means that professional educators as well as parents, community activists, and other citizens have a right to be fully informed and critical participation in creating school policies and programs for themselves and young people" (23).

Democratic schools are not merely about providing a democratic curriculum and a place for students to actively construct meaning in a caring atmosphere. They are also about the people who work in such schools having a primary place in the decision making about the school, including budgeting and hiring of staff. Teachers do not typically have the academic freedom to make changes and are not able to respond quickly to school planning and implementation due to the day-to-day demands of students, administration, and parents. There are also unpredictable crises and community resistance that intrude on a teacher's life.

Typically in the 1960s through the 1980s, teachers had autonomy while in their "ivory tower," their bastion of sanity, their classroom. With doors shut and alone with "their" students, teachers often did as they pleased with the curriculum. That is where decisions were made. Teachers were kings in their castles, and their word was law. The various reform efforts of the 1980s and 1990s blasted down those castle walls, and teachers suddenly were asked to make their teaching conform to curriculum demands of the state or to conform to high-stakes tests. As Apple and Beane (1995) proclaim:

> Even the most casual observers cannot help but notice that this right has been seriously eroded over the past several decades as curriculum decisions and even specific curriculum plans have been centralized in state and district offices of education. The consequent "deskilling" of teachers, the redefinition of their work as the implementation of others' ideas and plans, is among the most obvious, and unbecoming, examples of how democracy has been dissolving in schools. (56)

To counteract the dissolution of their power over their own classrooms, teachers turned to unions and union contracts to enlarge their sense of power and control, as well as to "upgrade" the profession. Local education associations vied with boards and administrators for control, rather than working together to form a democratic coalition for making decisions about schools. While unions appeared to give the teacher some semblance of democratic control (in that they at least voted for representatives and on contracts), it was a far cry from being able to create the kind of democratic schools spoken of by Glickman and Apple and Beane.

The structure of school in the past decades led to a culture of schooling that constituted a "hidden curriculum by which people learn significant lessons about justice, power, dignity, and self-worth" (Apple and Beane 1995:38). The hidden curriculum taught students they had no control over their own destiny and that they were not to be trusted with decisions about their own education and subsequent lives. It taught teachers they were decision makers only in their own classroom and in their particular relationships with students, but not in the overall governance of the school. Since state mandates have more or less destroyed that form of autocratic decision making, teachers have been asked instead to have more of a voice in creating the curriculum and creating constructivist instructional means by which students have some choice in their own education.

But part of the reform movements was the desire to bring a sense of empowerment to teachers in those decisions about statewide curriculum and testing, as well as decisions regarding how the mandates were to be met. Hence various attempts have been made to give teachers more autonomy within districtwide initiatives for reform. It has been a difficult transition from being king in one's own castle, small as that castle was, to being partners in decision making. Also difficult has been administrators relinquishing their role as decision makers. Many teachers who became administrators did so to become the hierarchical chieftains, to widen their castle territory, not to work democratically with teachers and parents.

Those tensions have been difficult for the professional educator, the parents, and the communities in general. Yet these tensions have brought opportunities for educational reform that would enhance democratic practices. One of the opportunities provided by many states has been the charter school laws that allow for development of teacher-led schools and have provided impetus for community-wide demands for innovative or more locally controlled schools. Another innovative approach that is having an impact is the development of teacher professional practices that have teachers as owners of their intellectual capital, "selling" their curricular knowledge and pedagogical expertise to a community group to form a school (Dirkswager 2002). This can certainly be a democratic venture if parents and other community members are perceived as capable of making their own decisions regarding the education of their own children.

The concept of democracy in our times means many things to different people. Generally, there has been a departure from the concept of early America. Alexis de Tocqueville in the 1830s wrote of early American concepts of democracy. He was an astute observer of human nature and of what made the American experiment work. According to de Tocqueville, popular sovereignty works when the numbers of people and the geographic area are small, preferably akin to the township of early New England states. In these townships, decision making was relatively successful due to the fact reason was informed by firsthand knowledge and the fact that "consequences of choice are readily visible, choosing well seems worth the time and effort; good results evoke personal pride" (Mansfield and Winthrop 2002:lx).

The concerns of the local democratic group are generally modest in nature, and ambition therefore is within manageable bounds. For example, as in a local school district or community, the "majority will is guided by passion that is partly selfish, partly caring, and moderated by practical experience." Were a tyranny to occur, it would be "petty and intrusive." At this level the majority rule could be unjust, but it is usually "well-informed, animated by pride, relatively benign." Unlike a tyranny of a state or a national government, a local government board has the benefit of being guided by people who are reachable, in the open, and guided by interests closest to the everyday needs of people (Mansfield and Winthrop 2002:lx).

David Matthews (1996) believes that the American public has been excluded from public schools by the movement from local one-room schools toward consolidated school districts that adopted the factory model of the scientific managers of the early 1900s. As the educational establishment seized the role of decision making regarding what should be taught and what should be learned, the public became more and more alienated from public schools. For example, "a 1992 survey found that, while nearly 60 percent of Americans thought parents and other members of the community should have more say in allocating funds and deciding the curriculum, less than 15 percent of administrators and only 26 percent of teachers shared this view" (Matthews 2002:18). The public, excluded from the decision making in the schools, turned to the elected officials of the state government to gain some measure of control over schools; but this remote management meant that control was even further removed.

Hence, the charter laws that attempt to place the governance of a local small school back into the hands of the parents and the local teachers, both of which lost control as management of schools became more and more centralized. For local control to again match the America of de Tocqueville's time, small, local constituencies of community members, along with teachers who wish to regain autonomy, will have to exercise the prime decision making for a small learning community.

The charter laws, as they exist in many states, but especially in Minnesota, allow for parents and local teachers to be in control of schools. This renewal of the concept of popular sovereignty in education has brought about some interesting developments, one of which is the truly democratic school. These democratic schools not only create a structure and curriculum to allow for student choice and voice but develop a structure that allows for democratic governance to occur.

In developing these democratic schools, the promise is that there will be

> an open flow of ideas that enables people to be as fully informed as possible, faith in the collective capacity to create possibilities for solving problems, the use of critical reflection and analysis to evaluate ideas, concern for the welfare of others, concern for the dignity and rights of others, and an organization of social institutions to promote and extend the democratic way of life. (Apple and Beane 1995:20)

The problem is that educators have to undo a century of having had nonclassroom decisions made for them by scientific managers and now politicians. And the public has to take it upon itself to get involved in the decision making pertaining to the curricular and pedagogical methods perpetrated on its children. Decision making by teachers in budgetary matters, personnel matters, strategic planning, and marketing as well as in curriculum and pedagogy is a difficult orientation and requires a paradigm shift. As Glickman (2001) puts it, "democracy as a learning experience is messy and not a part of the educational culture" (57).

Apple and Beane (1995) also speak to the difficulty of renewing the democratic school: "The idea of widespread participation in school affairs as a feature of democratic schools is thus not as simple as inviting participation, because the right to 'have a say' introduces questions about how various viewpoints fit into the fragile equation balancing special interests and the larger 'common good' of the democratic community" (30). Local school control by parents and local teachers is not merely a matter of creating an opportunity for local voice. It is a matter of balancing local voice, national sentiment, local law, state law, and national law. If local majorities attempt to create a situation whereby the rights of a minority are abused, some other of the local entities or state agencies needs to intervene. This intervention has been in many ways a problem in creating rules and regulations that may actually become a tyranny to the local constituency. So the balancing act begins, and the tussle may demolish the local democratic structure. Balancing state and federal mandates with local interests becomes more difficult year by year.

If government is looked on as being from grass roots up, rather than from the Beltway down, perhaps there would be fewer mandates. Local tyrannies may erupt when there is no federal agency to enforce a more balanced series of actions, but the tyranny of the state is more insidious and more difficult to eradicate. When mandates are local, the majority rule may be unjust. But as de Tocqueville recognized, it is usually "well-informed, animated by pride, and relatively benign" (Mansfield and Winthrop 2002: lx). And if democratic principles are adhered to, such as speaking with openness of ideas, good comunication, deliberation, critical analysis, and reflection, then a local tyranny is less likely to occur than is a state or federal one.

Take, for example, the standards movement that for all intents and purposes has been totally removed from local control. When the federal government presumes to make the rules pertaining to standards and testing children, a more pernicious tyranny over educational rights of the majority cannot be imagined. Why can't local parents be the judges of whether a school is effective for their children? Why can't local teachers develop curriculum and pedagogy that the local parents choose for their children? Why can't parents and children have a voice in what happens to them?

They can, if the school is a small neighborhood school that has in place structures and organizations that allow for decision making by teachers on curriculum and personnel, and allows for parents to choose the school and have a voice in its everyday operation. If that school also has a democratic curriculum and pedagogy in place, then it comes closer and closer to the ideal espoused by John Dewey, Carl Glickman, James Beane, Michael

Apple, and Harry Boyte. We then would have a condition closely akin to the public schools that David Matthews (2002) says would be ideal and that actually existed in America as far back as de Tocqueville's time.

Democratic decision making elicits other problems. It opens the possibility that those antidemocratic ideas such as censorship, engineering consent, perpetuation of historic inequities, and individual Machiavellian power plays may occur. Keeping democratic deliberative methods in place, and monitoring and observing them will be easier on a local level than it is on a national scale. Petty despotism may occur. However, if the parents, children, and teachers that lead the schools are in agreement on democratic principles and the focus of the school, whenever a local tyranny takes place there ought to be enough citizens within and without the school that become aware of it. They then ought to call it to the attention of the other constituents.

Another potential problem with teacher-led schools is the need for teachers and parents to play a larger and more expansive role. This will not be for every educator or for every parent. Teachers will have more responsibilities. Parents will need to be more involved than simply participating in the local school board election. However, if a school is organized around the principles of democratic schools, is constructivist, is small, is representative of the nature of the neighborhood in which it resides, and is freed from national and state mandates, then it is possible for teachers to assume those roles. As Apple and Beane say about teachers who do run democratic schools:

> Rather than spending more of their time on administrative tasks, curricula, teaching, and evaluation that are disconnected from their students and from the communities that they serve, rather than continuing to reproduce the conditions that make so many of our most talented teachers and administrators feel frustrated in their day-to-day lives, they have decided to make a break. They have decided to devote their lives as educators to engaging in educational activity organized around democratic social and pedagogical principles in which they strongly believe. In other words, they have chosen to be exhausted as a result of something worthwhile. (8)

Such schools are being constructed or, in many cases, reconstructed. Not only the schools Glickman and Apple and Beane speak of in their books, but also the EdVisions Schools is developing teacher-led schools that involve decision making in all aspects of the educational venture. The past ideals of de Tocqueville and Dewey can definitely be a prologue to the future. However, this democratization process requires extraordinary efforts on the part of the committed few. Is it worth it? Is it working? The next chapters speak to those efforts.

CHAPTER 4

The Future in the Present:
The Visions of EdVisions

I must create my own system or be enslaved by another's.

— William Blake

The burning question of the twenty-first century will be whether new education arrangements that are democratic and collaborative in nature will in fact come to fruition. The trend toward teacher autonomy is moving leadership in new directions. What format will teacher leadership take? If the past will hold on to the future, as discussed in the first chapter, the model of individual leadership via principals and superintendents will continue; or, at best, principals will create conditions for some sort of shared leadership model. But there are other alternatives where teachers have the opportunity to be democratic leaders of schools via a contract between the school and a professional practice organization.

Why should a teacher leadership model be considered? Teachers play a vital role in providing instructional leadership because they are on the front line with the learners every day. They are in a unique position to see the needs of individual students and groups of students, have tried varieties of interventions, found some things that work and some things that don't, and know the time demands on their particular situation. To attempt to foist reform on teachers from above has always proven problematic.

Teachers are central to the push for school reform. But the only ways for a teacher to have an impact on school reform is to become an administrator or become a union leader and activist, both of which require leaving the classroom and hence having less direct effect on students.

When teachers are followers rather than leaders, innovation is less likely. Principals are seen as the bosses, teachers the workers. The school culture is one of isolation rather than collaboration. There is a sense of egalitarianism that stymies reform efforts by well-minded teachers who want to lead reform. Teachers accept this because many want others to make those decisions for them; many are willing to trade autonomy for security; teachers are typically not entrepreneurial and in fact see profit-making as an evil in the public arena; and most teachers probably feel that the decisions they make in the classroom are enough. Those who do not accept these terms leave the profession. Only in the "teacher as owner" model (Dirkswager 2002) is it possible to allow for the intellectual capital of the teacher to take precedence.

If teachers were owners of their intellectual capital, would they be able to manage schools? Lead reform efforts? Be accountable for results? Would teachers become entrepreneurial? These are the questions asked by people like Ted Kolderie of the Center for Policy Studies in St. Paul. These questions were behind the crafting of the charter school law in Minnesota. When the law created the opportunity for teachers to be in control of the whole school operation, the Minnesota law made it possible for "teacher-led schools" to come into existence. Some of the teacher–parent groups that founded charters created schools that still used the principal–teacher model—one person given the responsibility to "run" the school; or a management company was given control of budgetary decisions and curriculum decisions. But one organization created a different entity altogether to test the conditions as a means toward answering the questions above: that was Ed-Visions Cooperative.

The EdVisions Cooperative was created not only to give teachers control of schools but also to create a sense of entrepreneurship in the enterprise of education. Teachers managing their own schools still may have the same sense of "duty" and "obligation" that existed in a master contract format, but they did not necessarily create the sense of ownership and a sense of meeting consumer needs. The additional element of a worker's cooperative formed of like-minded educators to "sell" their intellectual capital to a group of citizens in the form of a small charter school provided a greater sense of ownership and enterprise missing in conventional situations.

The idea was that teachers as owners would provide democratic leadership that was not about wielding power but about mobilizing the largely untapped attributes of teachers to strengthen student performance by working collaboratively in a shared leadership capacity. Bridging standards and accountability with the actuality of student interaction would be possible. Teachers could create environments where students would be known as individuals, ensuring policies for reform were in conjunction with the realities of school on a daily basis.

Other possible outcomes of teacher leadership would be creating a professional community with professional standards policed and maintained by the professionals themselves. This would give teachers the same opportunity as other professionals to work for themselves rather than for others. This abandons the principle that teachers must be employees and therefore followers of administrator and board initiatives. This in turn challenges the assumption that leaders must be trained administrators with a whole new set of skills and competencies and that only trained leaders can lead reform. It also challenges the notion that bigger is better; that large bureaucracies and central offices with curriculum and finance experts are needed to manage large school systems.

Teacher ownership could offer new roles to teachers: having control over their own accountability for the learning programs; determining appropriate fees for their services; controlling the budget, compensation, supplies, technology, and human resources services; and designing their own performance evaluation processes. Potential changes for teachers would be improving opportunities in shaping the mission and vision of a school and having greater personal control over the daily operations of the school. The direct control of budget would allow for teachers to make the trade-offs between compensation for services and learning program needs. This would place a greater amount of accountability on the teachers for demonstrated competence and professional growth, as they would have to prove that the program does or does not enhance student performance.

Having such an entrepreneurial teacher professional practice in charge of the operation of schooling would theoretically have a number of implications. For example, the teachers in charge would have a different outlook on the students who are in their charge. They would be seen as clients, not captive-passive receivers of information. Clients have needs, and entrepreneurial teachers attempt to satisfy those needs if they wish to continue the client–professional relationship. Parents would also be seen as clients, not intruders on the "expert's" turf. Parents' needs would be paramount to the enterprise, or otherwise they would take their business elsewhere. Of course, that denotes choice of schools and professional practices available, but that is also a feature of the charter school movement.

The relationship between teachers and school boards would change dramatically from one of hiring and micromanaging teaching practices to one of entering into agreements with professionals to provide services. The board then is forced into the task of being responsible for student results and would concern itself more with hiring the right professional group, not micromanaging daily situations. The school board would also be responsible for providing and maintaining facilities and outsourcing other services, but it would not be in the position of hiring teachers and negotiating master contracts. Unions would not be needed in this scenario, although professional practice organizations could unite around issues of security, contract negotiations, and so forth. Collective bargaining is a given, as the professional practice sells itself and its members for the whole program. But the paradigm shifts from protection of individuals by the organization to professional growth and results as an organization, therefore having a component of inherent personal and professional growth that is generally not apparent in teacher unions.

Another paradigm would have to be shifted: that of teacher preparation institutions and how they prepare teachers for their "practice." Rather than preparing teachers to be part of a large impersonal network, teachers would have to be prepared for "selling themselves," first to a professional practice, then to a school board as a group to provide a specific program. Teachers are not taught to be entrepreneurial. Although a few graduate programs are becoming available to help teachers think more as professionals who have intellectual capital to sell (e.g., those at Arizona State, UCLA, Florida Southern, and the universities associated with the EdVisions Leader's Center), no preservice teacher preparation program as of this writing has created an innovative program preparing teachers to be anything other than employees.

The teachers (called advisers in EdVisions sites) that lead schools in this professional association have developed a unique relationship within a legal worker's cooperative. The cooperative utilizes a contract with each school to supply the personnel and the learning program to the school. This causes an educational entrepreneurship to replace master contracts. In turn, the cooperative "hires" associates to serve the schools (actually, invites members to become part of the association). The cooperative, then, is a professional practice similar to professional practices in the legal and medical fields, although in this case in a worker's cooperative rather than a limited liability corporation or other type of corporate structure.

Why a cooperative? Basically for three reasons: First, the cooperative concept is a well-known structure in rural Minnesota and Wisconsin, with practically all communities having members in some sort of cooperative association. Second, although the cooperative structure is considered to be a for-profit structure, profits generally are returned to sites or members as patronage refunds; therefore, the idea of large profits from public monies going to an outside group of investors is nullified. Third, the cooperative is by nature an organization that utilizes equitable structures of governance, with local associations making local decisions and an elected board making decisions for the whole.

The creation of the cooperative allowed for provision of services (e.g., medical insurance and human resources services) that would have been too costly for individual small schools. And the association acts as a professional growth association by providing staff development opportunities to each other. There is still local site-based management. The cooperative is not a management company. The cooperative structure allows for flexible and dynamic decision making. Each school site management team, made up of members, decides on whom it wishes to bring on board as a member in its school. The local site management team also has the right to dismiss members. The overall cooperative board generally does not embroil itself in local politics unless asked to take part.

The members "hired" at each site are given a one-year at-will letter of employment. There is no tenure. The association views tenure as a nonentrepreneurial roadblock to professionalism and growth. Teachers/advisers are expected to show their value on an ongoing basis.

Compensation is based on the following expectations: professional development plans developed and accomplished; tasks done at the school, those having to do with growth of the students being paramount; and their contribution to the school's growth and sustainability. In other words, it is based on client satisfaction.

A professional development plan with certain criteria is provided to each member. A personnel team at each site reviews it every year. Professional growth, tied to accountability of both teacher and student, is expected (see Newell 2002a).

This approach was determined to help professionals become growth oriented, to be entrepreneurial in attitude and child centered in whatever reforms they attempt. It is expected that in this accountability for professionalism that student and parent input be considered. Sites are encouraged to have parent advisory boards, student advisory boards, and parents and students on committees and to make use of parent and student surveys pertaining to the work of the teacher-advisers. The personnel team, composed of a majority of licensed personnel at the site, takes into consideration the student growth of those under guidance of a particular associate, the professional development plan, and the input of parents and students. Then a recommendation is made to the local school board to retain, recompensate, or not retain a member. The school board does not decide on a person-to-person basis but is informed by the cooperative site management team that the personnel delivering the learning program for next year will change, with an explanation included. If a member is asked to leave the local site, the cooperative board of directors is notified.

The site management team of member-owners makes decisions at the site. Not only personnel, as mentioned earlier, but also in curriculum and instruction, finance, community relations, parent involvement, and assessment. Committees are formed to prioritize the issues and report to the larger site management team, where the ultimate decision would be made.

The role of the school board changes dramatically in this new arrangement. School boards enter into contracts for educational services (learning program and personnel, in the instance of EdVisions Cooperative), transportation, food service, and building maintenance. The school board also is responsible for providing facilities, statutory obligations, setting policies, and, above all, verifying results. The teacher organization hired to produce results has complete control over how the program is delivered and funded. The structure of the teacher agency providing the services does not have to be organized as a democratic and equitable cooperative, but if all voices are to be heard equally, it is the best possible scenario.

This democratic committee structure places a great deal of pressure on the site management team, for in addition to instructing students, it is expected to gather and disseminate information pertaining to all aspects of managing a school among itself and the constituents. It is in these committees and in the larger site management team meetings where democratic school governance and the collaborative culture take place. It is in the working of these committees, their ability or inability to gather and share the necessary information, where community is built or where community can be destroyed. There is no principal at most of the EdVisions sites. There are no superintendents in any of the schools. All administrative duties are exercised in the previously described democratic structure.

A member of the association and local site management team may assume the responsibility for preparing the financial and student data for state reporting, but this member is "hired" to do so by the teacher-owners. Those duties may be outsourced, especially if there is no one on site willing or able to take on those tasks. The same may be said for other administrative duties, such as state bureaucratic sign-off procedures, special education needs, and transportation. In all cases, the persons to whom the duties are outsourced are under the direction and the will of the teacher-owners, not vice versa.

The benefit of this arrangement is the capability of a flexible and dynamic decision-making process. Members of the site management team may reverse previous decisions if found ineffective, even the next day if so desired. The group can call site management team meetings to react to parent concerns, to student concerns, and act on those concerns immediately. The group can react immediately to results from action research or to new learning from members whenever it can be seen as appropriate. There are no bureaucratic walls or hoops to jump through; just coming to consensus as a group around the same table.

The vision is there would be a flat management process with no hierarchy, allowing for true site-based management to occur. No waiting for the right principal to assume leadership—the teachers lead themselves. No waiting for district initiatives from above—the teachers lead themselves at each site. There would presumably be a focus on individual, collegial, and institutional improvement on the part of each member of the site teams. This would be accompanied by a respect for and a nurturing of the intellectual and leadership capacities of each person on staff. Couple this with the dynamic and flexible information sharing of available research in teaching practices, learning, and assessment, and you would have continued growth of educators via a professional association. And you would have a model of successful democracy in the community, as the process should mirror the town meeting process espoused by de Tocqueville and others as the central element in American democracy.

Not only does the model mirror what ought to be the decision-making process of communities in general, but it is also a very efficient model of delivering education to learners. Because there is neither midlevel nor high-level management, dollars are saved in salaries. At the Minnesota New Country School, the original model of the cooperative venture, there were 103 students (using 2002–2003 statistics), a budget of $1,050,000, of which $568,000 (61 percent) was used for member salaries. The average salary for full-time-equivalent (FTE) certified staff (less benefits) was $43,500 (approximately $4,000 above the state average), with noncertified staff averaging $27,200. Administrative services costs were $27,000 (2.16 percent), most of which went to staff stipends for assuming specific responsibilities. A portion of the budget amounting to 3 to 5 percent per year goes to technology upgrades. Yet, with all of that, New Country shows a general fund balance going into the 2003–2004 year of $275,000, or about 26 percent. This was in a time of economic woes, when over a third of the school districts in Minnesota were showing a negative general fund balance.

The staffing of the project-based school is, of course, different from that of the typical comprehensive high school. Each teacher is an adviser to seventeen to eighteen students and oversees their learning program. This is done via student interest-driven projects rather than delivery of courses (see Newell 2002b). It is not only in the governance model that such efficiency can be delivered; it also takes creative staffing patterns and learning models, as well as a staff willing to assume the collaborative committee work necessary.

Is this a model that educators can adopt? Are educators willing and able to take on the tasks necessary to manage democratic schools? Can they overcome the culture of nonempowerment and take on themselves the mantle of collective aspirations, collaborative activities, and deliberative democracy? Can cultural attitudes and collective memory be overcome? If proper processes are incorporated into the learning community culture, if the teacher-leaders will master the collaborative components, then the vision of EdVisions Schools can be fulfilled.

CHAPTER 5

Educational Collaboratives:
The Five Facets of Mastery

> Daring ideas are like chessman moved forward. They may be beaten, but they may also start a winning game.
>
> —Goethe

As mentioned previously, most teachers function primarily in dependent or independent modes. They work within systems in which almost all educational policies are predetermined. Typically they have very little say over those policies and limited or no access to decision making (Smylie 2000). As a major consolation, however, they enjoy the supreme comfort of being masters of their fate when they close the door of their classroom. There they rule supreme. There they can shut out all the political rhetoric and just teach their students.

Well, not quite. Presently high-stakes testing is intruding, directing and controlling. Security issues and zero tolerance are compelling a new, more self-conscious kind of vigilance. Accountability hangs over the classrooms like a generic pall. In other words, administrative overrides and intrusions have become increasingly the norm. Teachers have found their traditional sanctuary invaded. Their independence has been steadily eroded. The teacher is becoming more dependent than independent overall.

The problem is good professionals thrive on opportunities (Brown and Cornwall 2000). Take away initiatives, and teachers languish. They act like automatons. They go about their daily business like workers on a factory floor. Survival, not growth, becomes the focus. Asked again and again to return to rote, and to teach to tests, they become expensive drill sergeants. There is less and less room and time to teach concepts and comprehension, which would bring some intelligence to the production line. But one of the special wonders of historical cycles is that just as we appear to be encountering the law of diminishing returns, another pattern appears. It surfaces as an alternative and argues that rather than stay with or slightly improve the status quo, use what may be the end of something to perceive the beginning of something quite different and challenging, such as EdVisions Schools.

As mentioned in chapter 1, educational relationships, structures, and governance are showing signs of increasingly becoming collaborative (Hill, Pierce, and Guthrie 1997; Murphy and Doyle 2001; Dirkswager 2002). Moreover, such interdependence appears to have the potential to affect the total process: administration, instruction, and measurement (National Commission 1999). EdVisions Schools have developed a high degree of collaboration that exhibits a transformation. So that this discussion is anchored in specifics, here is a matrix that spells out a series of developmental trends and concrete examples of teacher collaboration, which already have surfaced in key areas (see table 5.1).

Table 5.1.   The Collaborative Spectrum

Activities	Traditional	Transitional	Transformational
1. New hires	Little or no say	Sit in on interviews	Select new hires
2. Instruction	Already chosen	Few alternatives	Cooperative learning
3. Collegiality	Limited	Committees	Team managed
4. Student roles	Controlled	Some variety	Negotiated
5. Parental roles	PTO	Involvement	Partnerships
6. Schedules	Prescribed	Altered	Fluid
7. Finances	No involvement	Budget review	Shared accountability
8. Professional development	Chosen	Half/Half	Teacher choice
9. Tech. choices	No consultation	Committee input	Team choice
10. Teacher evaluation	Principal	Principal and faculty	360-degree self-evaluation
11. Lesson plans	Individual	Generic	Collaborative
12. Student work	Individual	Interdisciplinary	Collective
13. Decision making	Administrator	Shared	Collaborative
14. Student evaluation	Tests	Tests/Reflection	Portfolio
15. Best practices	Identified	Tested in classroom	Action research

One of the values of the matrix is that it visually compels the recognition of the interconnectedness of change. Specifically, three interlocking patterns appear. First, there is the necessity to integrate the three major components of the educational process: administration, instruction, and measurement. Failing that, each third does not directly contribute to or reinforce the other parts and thus sets up a fragmentary tug of war between components that should be harmonized. The problem is finding the glue of commonality. Adversarial relationships between administrators and teachers have been compounded by equally testy relationships between legislators and educators in the name of accountability. The net result is the key parts of education are often at odds with each other. But in a collaborative environment, which is dedicated to bringing together what is often asunder, horizontal relations are easy and common.

But the second pattern is perhaps even more striking. As the collaborative takes hold and as teachers enjoy a greater centrality, the standards of collaboration increasingly become the same for everything and everyone. The standards for judging students, teachers, parents, and programs are uniformly tasking. Accountability comprehensively applies equally to finances as to passing mandated tests. In other words, a collaborative structure compels mutuality. There is no special set of standards for teachers apart from standards for students. They are one and the same. Teachers now freer to enjoy decision making have to extend it to students and parents. Collaborative means everybody. Access is total. All is transparent. There are no secrets and no deceptions. Everything is there for all to see and know and act upon.

The third matrix, alas, is not inevitable, even in EdVisions sites. The spectrum stakes out a final collaborative state, but that is not guaranteed. In other words, another value of the matrix is that it accommodates the prospect of different paths and conclusions. It makes clear that the final version as pictured is not set in stone. Indeed, what it does produce is the consideration of interventions. The key focus is the transitional state.

Three options immediately present themselves. The first is to make the transitional state permanent. Administrators and school boards may conclude that is as far as things go. They may see the handwriting on the wall and conclude that collaboration jeopardizes control and direction.

That way leads to anarchy because no one is in charge. It is obviously a teacher, student, parent, and community-centered giveaway. It may be tolerated in part and up to a point, but its momentum must be arrested; otherwise those officially responsible are guilty of abdicating their responsibilities. It is time for Pharaoh once again to assume the burden of leadership. No martyr will happily or willingly give up his or her stigmata. Besides, once pacified the old order can be gradually and even slyly restored.

The second option is indeed transitional for administrators. Through enlightenment or opportunism, they may decide that collaboration is in fact the wave of the future. Principal–teacher partnerships are gradually emerging, and, in fact, have occurred already in a number of schools. One of those to receive national attention is the McCosh Elementary School in Chicago.

The arrangement is one of shared power or distributed leadership. A collaborative team administers the schools; the teachers on the team remain in the classroom; most developments for change are teacher initiated; the principal is internally the primary facilitator and externally the link to the district and the school board.

Where this setup exists, it appears to work well. But three serious problems have surfaced. First, principals who are willing to share leadership are frequently not popular with other principals. In fact, they may have to deny many of the central assumptions of their certified training and be willing to accept a leadership and management arrangement and style, which many find belittling. Then, too, they have to stay the course. If they leave, they are often replaced by a principal, who, like our first option, is a throwback (Elmore 1996). Indeed, the newcomer may have been chosen to regain lost ground.

The other problem is that teachers may demand more. They may ask for higher pay, more assistance in the classroom, time off, change in title, and so forth. A few of the teachers may even question whether the principal is needed at all. They are doing all the work and making all the decisions. He is merely a token head. They thus may believe that they are doing more than just being teachers and such differentials should be separately recognized and rewarded. If granted, the positions may become competitively desirable. But most likely the district citing problems of equity across the board will refuse to grant separate status and pay. The danger then is that the partnership may become shaky and even dissolve.

The third option is genuinely radical. It rests on the assumption, borne out of decades of observing the lack of genuine and comprehensive school change, that authentic and lasting transformation cannot occur within the current structure. For substantial change to occur, it has to happen outside the current system. This lesson was not lost on business nearly a decade ago (Christensen 2000). After watching a number of new ventures being internally consumed shortly after being launched, a number of corporations decided to spawn new initiatives as separate and independent companies outside and apart from parental environs. Those generally fared much better, survived, and provided the company with a much-needed diversification of products and services and of income. In education, the charter school movement and EdVisions Cooperative have provided the viable alternative structure.

Not all charter schools are inherently adventuresome, innovative, or collaborative; many are in fact even more conservative than schools in the same district. But where collaboration has taken hold, it has done so in charter schools that at least offer a tabula rasa, or break from past patterns (Charter Friends Network 2001). Indeed, the EdVisions schools fully embody and on a daily basis live the learning life of the transformational agenda (Thomas 1996). Although one can visit the first school to adopt the model, the Minnesota New Country School, and simply copy or replicate what is going on there, that approach might be a disservice to the difference of elsewhere. It might make more sense to distill the essences of collaboration so that it can accommodate multiple applications and give us a tool whereby we may judge where schools are in their transformation.

In the EdVisions schools and elsewhere, collaboration has minimally at least five facets. And each facet requires teacher–administrators to change their roles and wear different hats. The five dimensions are:

- the collective,
- the consultative,
- the coaching commitment,
- consensuality, and
- creating community.

The *collective*, like steel bands that hold a barrel together, focuses on forging commonality. Specifically, it engages the big picture of what we are collectively about and forges a common focus. The definition and redefinition of vision and mission are both institutional and individual. Indeed, it begins with each member of the collaborative composing his or her own mission statement and work range. These are shared and aggregated upward to yield the organizational version.

The collective focus also requires that the larger issues of the future of education and future of the teaching profession be engaged. Such professionalism of learning also has to become a part of the vision and mission statement because it identifies, on the one hand, the context within which the collaborative mission has meaning and, on the other hand, binds all teachers together in common causes. The awareness of the debates about standards, high-stakes mandated testing, accountability issues, and so forth, surrounding and emanating from that larger professionalism, is anchored by becoming members of key teacher organizations and subscribing to journals. The application of the collective focus appears minimally in the collective discussion of learning plans, the development of learning rubrics for common assignments (Andrade 1999), and the regular review and examination of student work. As these rigors take hold, other collective activities are sure to be suggested as the collaborative approach receives further socialization and affirmation.

The *consultative* requires every member to function as a consultant to all other internal clients of the collaborative—teachers, students, parents, specialists, and others (Ginsberg, Johnson, and Moffett 2001). The relationship is attitudinal. It stresses inquiry, assessment, and problem solving—what in business is called customer service. But its principal preoccupation is with research and data sources. The collaborative consultant is invariably knowledgeable about current research and findings. Whenever possible, the hiring process factors in the need for research specializations not available among current staff.

The two principal applications of this research commitment are undertaking schoolwide research by the professional staff and the training of all students (and if appropriate, parents) in research methodologies and design (Reason and Bradbury 2000). Monthly seminars are held for the presentations of teacher and student research projects and findings. Those involving community projects are carefully reviewed, and suggestions are made for their being presented in appropriate venues. Other research is reviewed for presentation at conferences or offered for publication. Thus, this micro-application honors the larger issue of the profession.

The *coaching commitment* requires that both teachers and students be defined as unfinished learners or unlearners. Each teacher and student has a coach or mentor (Robbins 2001). That individual may or may not be a teacher in the program. He or she may be a parent, a business leader, a college professor, or an elected official. The function of coaching for the staff is to encourage and structure three dimensions of continuous improvement. The first involves evaluation of performance. Ideally, that evaluation should be initially private and not be a part of an official process so that the individual teachers can examine how they are multiply perceived. Then a coach reviews the same data with the individual involved, if necessary playing the role of devil's advocate. Finally, all the results of all the evaluations are shared and compared so that the cumulative effect of the collaborative can be assessed and so that common denominators of deficiency can be identified for professional development.

Each teacher and student, with their respective coaches, also develops professional development plans (Thomas 1996). No official approval is required. Ideally the plan is filed on the school website and thus is available and accessible to all. All the activities and interventions are entered and, as accomplished, described and evaluated. The coach adds input at each stage.

Finally, the coach works on governance. A participatory environment is not guaranteed. It requires constant and full use lest it rust. Coaches thus encourage resourcefulness and increasing interdependence. Specifically, teachers and students are expected increasingly to become self-starting, self-organized, self-sustaining, self-perpetuating, and self-actualizing. But they also are encouraged to strengthen and manage interdependence, which is often frustrating and time-consuming. The goal is to create a collectivized individual.

The *consensual* demands that collaborative decisions are not arrived at by majority vote but by consensus. The value of that process is its total inclusivity. No one is left out. No one is unheard. Everyone is on board, happily or not, but they have had their say. To be sure, it requires more time and energy. The risk is finally reaching agreement only because of exhaustion. Control is not easily given up. This means that teachers and many professionals initially are often not effective at the collaborative process just as students are not good at democratically managing their own education without practice. Student government is often a token arrangement compared to the opportunity to manage learning through negotiation, deliberation, and consensus. Collectively teachers and staff must meet to discuss and share various effective ways of benign abandonment when it appears others are not in agreement.

The ultimate yield of the transformational collaborative is to create a learning and humane *community*. It involves both social and intellectual behavior modification. All learn to live, study, and manage collaboratively together, employing a governance structure that they helped create and that they must sustain. The students emerging from this community will be superior to their teachers in achieving consensus. They may also be more assertive politically. But certainly they will have the cultural milieu of a democratic society from which to learn applications of democratic procedures à la Boyte (2000), Glickman (2001), and Apple and Beane (1995).

The school community in a collaborative environment is continuous with the larger outside community. Happily, charter schools have to be more sensitive to that extension because they are political creations. Often, in fact, they were opposed initially or approval was begrudging. Charter school staff is aware that there are many citizens on the sidelines cheering them on to failure. It is thus not accidental that many collaborative charter schools opt for service learning as a way of bridging school and community.

In many ways, it is even beneficial for teachers and staff to experience such precariousness. They realize that their survival is neither automatic nor guaranteed. They are not complacent. They remain vigilant. In many ways, they exist in a more competitive environment than most established schools. In fact, they are always in danger of closing, especially if they fail to manage their finances well (Brown and Cornwall 2000). Not unexpectedly, their strongest supporters are not educators but members of the business community.

In summary, then, are there any downsides to this collaborative paradise? First, it is far from being a universal solution. Most teachers would not wish to be involved. They have a traditional view of their role, and they do not wish to take on the additional dimensions of administration and research. They also have a somewhat irrational need for someone to be in charge of the front office. They cannot conceive of themselves as running a school. It is estimated that less than 25 percent of all teachers would accept a leadership role; we would put it at 10 percent.

Many students also would not be interested, although because of home and online schooling that may change. But generally students are used to set classes with instructors and being told what to do. They generally are not given any or are given very few opportunities to learn and research on their own with little or no supervision. Although given that opportunity, the numbers that would be interested might increase substantially.

Most parents would not be interested. They would be fearful that their children would not be properly prepared for college or work. They are wary of experimental arrangements and of their children being used as guinea pigs. Above all, many parents are generally unwilling or reluctant to become heavily involved in the instructional or administrative aspects of a school's program. That alone may make them worry about the professionalism of the entire operation.

Hardly any administrators would be attracted to a collaborative because there is no room for them to be top dog. Sadly, many already have publicly and privately derided the collaborative governance structure to interested parents in their districts and issued vague warnings of inadequacy. They also have predicted that the new collaboratives are fly-by-night or short-term operations that will fold and leave children stranded.

The members of the community are a mixed bag. Those influenced politically by the school boards and administrators of the school district are wary. A few who have attended the open houses of the school are cautiously supportive. The most enthusiastic group are the businesspeople who are enormously impressed by the willingness to accept cost controls, even if it means that the students and teachers accept custodial chores to save money or stay within budget.

Clearly, then, the collaborative model is not for everyone. Nor was it designed to be. Three motives drive the model. A minority of teachers has a strong desire to create a different way of crafting and sustaining a learning community. And as long as that passion, borne of discontent, is there, experimentation with alternatives will continue. That strong desire is accompanied by the recognition that if any design is to succeed, it cannot occur or take hold within a system that is constitutionally hierarchical and controlling. New soil is required for different crops. Finally, there is general acceptance that everything about the collaborative will be small and follow human scale. The number of students will be limited; the ratio of teachers to students will be high; there will be no separate administration; teachers will be paid minimally at the level of the traditional districts or higher; the entire school can gather for a meeting and everybody will know everybody.

In short, the entire operation is conceived as a minority model. It is not meant for everyone. It is not transferable to a traditional school structure. It is not intended to change or reform all public education. All it asks is that it not be harassed or derided, be allowed to go about its business of offering a genuine alternative, and be judged by its accomplishments and outcomes.

Because it is never easy to overcome a culture of educating that has kept teachers from having democratic control of a collaborative learning community, taking the risk to create such cultures inevitably leads to problems of process, enactment, follow-through, and just plain old human error. In establishing learning communities that are indicative of the collective, the consultative, the coaching commitment, and consensuality, the EdVisions sites indeed have discovered problems and promises. It is not an easy road. Is it worth it? Let the practitioner voices speak.

CHAPTER 6

Obstacles and Opportunities: Feedback from Practitioners

The highest reward of a person's toil is not what they get for it, but what they become by it.

—John Rankin

Creating a collaborative culture from scratch and maintaining its momentum is no easy task. Indeed, it is probably as difficult as putting an effective team together. Teams are made, not born; we do not have to be taught how to take but how to share. The downside of trying out new relationships and structures early on is trial by error. The upside is a better understanding and respect for the complexities and dynamics involved. In short, it is a learning and growth experience.

But precise feedback was needed for many reasons. EdVisions' credibility was on the line. Could the culture, in fact, be created and maintained in the first place? If so, at what price? What recurrent and even generic obstacles had to be overcome? Could knowing those be anticipated and dislocation minimized? Could training in advance minimize the obstacles and optimize the opportunities? Finally, how could this course of reform be recommended in good conscience to those outside EdVisions without showing both its blemishes and beauties?

So a self-study was initiated. Staff members with at least two years' experience in EdVisions schools from four sites were given an open-ended survey. They were asked to reflect on the five aspects of implementing a collaborative culture: the consensual, collective, consultative, coaching component, and community. Ten staff members responded. This chapter presents an analysis of the results. (A complete rendering of all comments appears in appendices A and B.)

CONSENSUAL

The primary obstacle in implementing consensus is use of time. The majority of teachers working in classrooms do not give time to making decisions about funding, personnel issues, overall program concerns, and the myriad of committee and board meetings that democratic leaders deal with weekly. And they do not have to listen to everyone else around a table for interminable minutes getting viewpoints on all those decisions. "There are too many meetings," says one of the practitioners, and it leads to stress when confronted with time away from family and other concerns. One practitioner said that "coming to consensus after listening to all voices in the committee and full staff meetings is tiring and exhausting and can be frustrating." Often many of the discussions are "on small issues or personal preferences" that "can interfere with the communal purpose." Like another practitioner says, "it is like herding cats—so many ideas and thoughts are presented—time does not allow for all the discussion needed."

When all voices are heard, and the ideas, concepts, and opinions pertaining to every decision must make the rounds, there will be a great deal of time taken up. The organizing of disparate thoughts and searching for clarity is another fairly obvious problem in reaching consensus. Not every practitioner has the same feeling for every issue, or perhaps many have different issues about which they are emotional. If the emotional "trigger" issue is not high on the agenda of the others, they may have to listen anyway to keep the circle process going.

Time is not the only issue. Coming to consensus is difficult because "staff may lack knowledge, experience, and information needed to make sound decisions." For many teachers operating in the democratic arena for the first time, they are not trained in skills needed for consensus. "An effective decision-making body requires skills and a high level of personal awareness that is not well developed in most people," said another of the teacher-leaders. "We need training/understanding on how to implement this process effectively," said another. To teachers unused to leading by utilizing consensus decisions, frustration mounts when their colleagues do not interact professionally and in a democratic way.

One of the outcomes of this inability to interact is "people who speak 'more' and 'louder' and that intimidate some from speaking out." This can lead to one of the more troubling aspects; "it is easy to fall into a power structure and may have a tendency for people to align themselves with the power." If the teacher is not a leader and has a tendency to lay back and let others talk, or not attend meetings, certain individuals, the louder voices, can take control and make the majority of the decisions.

Educators who are more inclined to think things through, who want information before reacting, who are more "laid back" may be "bulldozed" by those who speak loudly, overreact, or withhold information to further their cause. In short, simply by applying the democratic model of decision by consensus does not ensure that it will in actuality take place. And even when the process is carried out without any rancor or power plays, it can be a long, time-consuming process.

The majority of the comments on the promises of using the consensus model had to do with having a voice. "Great to have my voice heard and to hear other voices," said one practitioner. "It empowers all to be involved, heard, and to continue growth," said another. This having a voice at the table results in three very important outcomes: presentation of new ideas, the building of community, and the modeling of democratic action for students.

"We have some great brainstorming that evolves into great new ways of doing things," was the comment of one teacher-leader. Another said, "Everyone is a key stakeholder and we lose the perception of 'us versus them.'" "Everyone backs the decision," another said, "since everyone was a part of making it," and yet another commented, "Everyone shoulders the positive or negative results."

This building of community can be as strong, or stronger, than the division that may take place with "louder voices." The promise of creating a positive culture of consensus becomes obvious: When educators undertake to listen to all voices before making a decision, a feeling of closeness, of "being in this together," and of "oneness" is possible. Most people like to have all voices heard, and it appears to make the decision more powerful in terms of becoming upheld by everyone being "on board."

It also models the democratic school for the students. "It is democracy in action. The civic action is easier to instill in students when they actually get to practice it. It is easier to teach because those who teach it also get to practice it as well," said one of the practitioners. In addition, "the work and collaboration of the staff serves as a role model to students of interpersonal interaction and communication." These are powerful statements and link directly to the thoughts, opinions, and actions spoken of by Dewey, Boyte, and Apple and Beane. The democratic school becomes possible by the interactions required by building consensus to manage the school itself.

And it makes everyone a stakeholder, not merely a worker. Everyone has the opportunity to have firsthand involvement in discussions leading to decisions. Some key quotes form the comments of the responders: "Everyone is a key stakeholder," "It forces people into professional decisions that otherwise are made by others," and "If people are comfortable saying what they mean, stakeholders have the opportunity to have a great deal of input."

Being able to have input into the daily undertaking of educating students raises the bar for everyone involved, and empowers teachers to make decisions. Teacher-advisers in this situation can see firsthand what results from their decisions. For the most part, that appears to be a positive aspect of coming to consensus.

The fact that coming to consensus brings with it the positive outlook of stakeholders means that the school is going to have a better culture than a school with very little "buy-in" on the part of the staff. The togetherness that can be fostered by a culture of consensus is very powerful, giving the culture of the school an atmosphere of interaction and camaraderie, which means that students and parents will be valued and welcomed as part of the team. This in turn leads to the continued development of the collective focus.

COLLECTIVE

The preceding comments ought to be kept in mind when considering the problems in creating and maintaining the collective focus. Some of the same comments given were also made concerning the problems of creating consensus. For example, "The development of an inclusive community requires skills and a level of personal awareness that is not well developed in most people" refers to the lack of interpersonal skills to build consensus. It appears that many of the teacher-leaders in the EdVisions schools also feel unprepared for maintaining a school's collective focus.

Also, "the division of staff over small issues/personal preferences can interfere with the communal purpose" was another comment. And, again, the issue of time: "It requires a great deal of time and effort to get all on the same page," said another practitioner. Other issues mentioned include making decisions when members were not present, divisions between staff with licenses and those without, manipulators who frustrate the process, and decisions that "morph and change with individual situations, causing confusion and or resentment."

Another problem in many schools, especially start-up charter schools, is the hiring of new staff. Creating and maintaining a common focus is difficult in schools because the "workforce" comes to a school from different places with different philosophies. Even in EdVisions Schools that are for the most part created schools by a founding group with a mission, hiring new staff becomes a major chore. If the hired staff were not with the group from the beginning, they have to be incorporated into a culture of the collective—they have to buy in to the vision and mission. If they do not, then problems creating or maintaining the focus will surface.

Also, as mentioned by the practitioners, divisions between staff may occur over small issues and over roles people are supposed to take. If job descriptions are not clear, decision making may appear a power grab. Decisions are often made without all voices at the table, again making it appear as if those absent voices are not valued. And, again, the "loud voice" syndrome rears its ugly head. It is true that educators are not trained to work together at building common focus and consensus building while in their initial teacher preparation programs. Therefore, this skill must be developed by the group while they are actually managing a school.

The promises or positives in creating a collective focus are that "the mission is revisited often and is the basis for most decisions. If the mission is foremost in the minds of the group while making decisions, then common focus can be maintained. It does take strong-minded leaders who are willing to shoulder the responsibility for maintaining that vision."

The togetherness brings about an exciting venue in which to work. One practitioner put it this way: "Common vision is incredibly exciting! Students and parents see that vision and adopt it quickly because it is coming as one voice. Strong spirit!" When that spirit is strong, then students and parents see easily that the school has focus and togetherness. Having a common focus and the willingness to work toward that common goal is one of the elements of a strong school.

It also appears that the practitioners recognize the need to build community by continued reflection and listening to all voices. "All must take responsibility for decision making and the consequences," said one respondent. However, the community "must be kept small," making the goal more realizable.

Another comment that brings teacher leadership into focus is that working together and making decisions together "forces continued reflection on vision and mission that traditionally was easily lost in the shuffle." The collective allows for the continual revisiting of the mission and vision, giving student-centered decision making a strong base. A strong collective can keep everyone involved in going in the same direction. The common focus is strengthened and maintained by continual consensual activity. This certainly is a major strength when juxtaposed with the typical large staff of a comprehensive high school in which the teachers are Lone Rangers.

CONSULTATIVE

The problems with implementing the consultative aspect of the culture are similar in nature to the consensual and the collective. The frustration of dealing with students, parents, and other faculty is physically draining and time-consuming. Helping each other continually learn, do the action research, do the staff development, listen to those who have learned, is a time-consuming task. "The constant new learning can be overwhelming and exhausting," said one respondent.

Also, untrained teachers are asked to be mentors to new staff and to their colleagues. For many teachers new to the leadership role, "it is difficult to judge what the needs are and when someone is ready for the 'next step.'" There is uncertainty around knowing and deciding what colleagues need to improve the school. The confrontation it would take to get other staff to listen, to do the reading, to go to workshops, is difficult when all are perceived to be equals, and some do not believe they have to improve or change. And, as one teacher-leader said, "Confrontation with those who are not following through is more difficult with a group than it is with principal to teacher." Certainly dealing with a hierarchy where one person is placed in control would be easier. But then the promises of implementing the consultative would not be present.

Although it is tiring, painful, and often frustrating to build the consultative element into the school culture, it can also be an enlightening and uplifting experience when staff members support each other in their growth. "It is refreshing and revitalizing"; "This allows me to be more effective and satisfied"; "We see that we are always learning"; "We are actively involved in the profession—personal growth is greater." These comments from practitioners support the excitement that can come from whole-staff support of individual growth and the focus it provides if in conjunction with building consensus and the collective.

In addition, "the mentality of life-long learning with reflective practice gives students and staff the skills and confidence to adapt to new situations and environments." The consultative facet of collaboration creates a whole new environment in teacher-managed schools. "Reflection allows for us to see serious areas for change," said another practitioner. "The constant new learning can be exciting and gives a much better understanding of all aspects of education and the education system," said another. And, "there were a lot more frustrating unknowns when I was in the traditional school system" was another comment.

Reflective practices are essential in a democratic process, and when the collective group puts emphasis on the consultative aspect, thoughts and feelings such as "effective," "confidence," "satisfied," and "personal growth" will be more prevalent. This excitement and the knowledge gained by consulting with each other appear to be aspects of the education profession missing in traditional settings.

COACHING COMMITMENT

The coaching commitment is akin to the consultative aspect and has sim-ilar problems in being initiated and maintained. "It requires care and a high level of interpersonal communication for consistent and construc-tive criticism," and "teachers are often too nice to confront each other at the expense of the mission. . . . the tendency is to not get at the deeper is-sues," are some comments made by respondents. It requires openness and willingness to be coached, it requires good interpersonal skills on the part of everyone. Confrontation is difficult to either do or accept, and the attempt to build a good coaching element into a school may lead to frus-tration and time investment people are not willing to undertake.

Most of the practitioners surveyed were involved in the creation of the school and all of the work that entailed. From the standpoint of those of us who were technical assistants to the sites, it appears as if the coaching commitment, even more so than the consultative attitude, was not a high priority. The unwillingness of teacher-practitioners to take the initiative to coach others, when not trained or holders of the princi-pal license, appeared to be very strong.

But just as strong was the unwillingness of many to accept coaching. "It doesn't work so well for people who believe they are perfect, are afraid of change or criticism, or unable to comment on others," and "evaluating and supporting each other requires openness to new learn-ing and understanding. . . . it is hard and can be painful." "A majority of the staff may never buy in to the great ideas of one of the staff."

As can be seen from these comments, creating a coaching culture in a small, democratic school is not enough. A structure has to be built, and the collective, consensual, and consultative facets must be sup-ported by a process that acculturates new members and supports expe-rienced members. When such a structure exists, the coaching commit-ment can be very powerful.

The promises of implementing the coaching commitment lead to growth as an educator and as a role model. Although there is a general unwillingness to accept coaching, some practitioners surveyed pointed out strengths and positive aspects about the coaching commitment. "Looking honestly at self and others in job performance can lead to a deeper understanding and appreciation of self and others." This can lead to becoming "more comfortable interacting with peers." In addition, small groups of teacher-leaders "can act as cheerleaders for others."

Small staff can all participate in the same workshops, discuss the details, and, by consensus, come to conclusions as to how best affect student learning. The interaction builds camaraderie, consistency, and an "ongoing movement toward self-actualization" as an educator. Building the coaching commitment into the school process can cause positive growth both institutionally and individually.

COMMUNITY

The element of community building elicited more responses than any of the other elements of the collaborative culture. The obstacles include "the reality of pulling together along the same path," which "is more difficult than the idea. Whereas we may share the common vision and mission, we may not agree on the same path to actualize these." Another difficulty is that "people are not accustomed to being listened to, or being responsible for speaking well and ethically." Therefore, "working together is hard and you don't always get what you want," causing "some stakeholders not being involved enough to feel passionate and empowered." Getting a large number of people together to go in the same direction is a frustrating and time-consuming task.

Another problem is that communication skills concerning democratic action on the level of the "town meeting" are not inherent in groups of citizens, even if they are united around a cause. That requires "a deep involvement in the lives of those around us." "A traditional school staff can hide in their classrooms, but we (students and staff) are in the open, warts and all, for all to see and judge—we live in glass houses," commented a respondent. It would be easy to retreat and opt for older methods of creating a hierarchy and giving power to decision-makers. But that destroys the closeness, the camaraderie, the dynamism of the democratic decision-making process.

Acculturating new staff or students into the community also proves difficult. "It is hard for students and some parents who have had difficulties in school to believe in adults and schools as a community," said one respondent. "Students are often uncomfortable with adults caring for them because they have not had that in the past," said another practitioner. Overcoming these problems presents new forms of parent and student interaction, building relationships differently and on different premises than in the traditional school setting, where the authoritarian model is the norm.

Also, one of the problems of building and maintaining community is the inability of a busy staff to find time to celebrate their successes. "We sometimes get too focused on pressing issues and what needs to be improved and not on what has been accomplished. We don't celebrate accomplishments enough." It is difficult to maintain community when all you are doing is trouble-shooting.

However, there are promises in the teachers democratically leading their schools in regard to community. Some positive comments made by the practitioners include "We like each other. We really do. It really is a nice place to spend my day," and, "Our community gives a sense of belonging and support for the development of skills and abilities."

Other comments speak to the strong community built in most of the EdVisions schools: "A well-functioning community means most problems are talked out and dealt with before they give rise to gossip, infighting, long-term disputes," and "the community develops important methods for relating to people and serves to benefit everyone. It gives space for further progress." "Advisers build great relationships. We celebrate and mourn together as a community."

Not only adviser-teachers and students build great bonds, but families do as well: "After working with a family for a couple of years, the relationship is incredibly strong and supportive." And student-to-student bonds grow: "The students watch out for each other—they hug each other after breaks and weekends and are glad to be back in school." Another respondent said, "Students see themselves as valuable members of the community and that being a citizen is as much a responsibility as a right. Many are extremely involved in and out off the school. As they get older, their view of community expands."

As other practitioners noted, "We can integrate school with the greater community—it is not school on an island," which leads to the ability to "teach a real social curriculum." Many comments were made pertaining to the interaction with the community and the potential for "contributing strengths and sharing burdens"

Overall, the community building that goes on with the EdVisions schools program, one that allows for advisers and students to interact as adults about learning not only curriculum but learning about life from each other and building common bonds. The following two quotes sum up this strength of community building: "It has been good for students to interact more with each other—they become more proactive in difficulties, and they often take the lead in conversations." "The traditional relationships are to a great extent broken—many relationships with staff to staff, staff to student, and student to student can and do become more personal than in a traditional school. We have the opportunity to be a major adult figure in many students' lives."

Creating a strong community can be very invigorating. The terms used by the practitioners to describe their communities are tremendously powerful: "celebration," "liking each other," "watching out for each other," "a sense of belonging," "support," "problems talked out," "giving space," "incredibly strong and supportive family relationships," "students as real members of the community," "involved," "sharing strengths," "sharing burdens," "opportunities for new learning," "integrating school with the greater community," lead to relationships between students and staff that are "incredibly strong and safe." More than anything else, these comments ought to sell the EdVisions model.

This last statement says it all: "When a child feels safe and cared for, [his or her] learning increases exponentially." That is what building community is all about. It is the first and the last, the first thing needed to be done, and the culmination of all of the five elements of the collaborative culture: build good relationships among all stakeholders, especially students and faculty, and the other elements will come more easily.

In addition to considering problems and promises of the five aspects of a collaborative culture, practitioners were also asked to respond to four statements pertaining to teachers managing their schools. The statements put to them were as follows:

1. Being a member of a democratic school has provided a more cohesive and integrated sense of purpose, goals, and measurements of success for our school.

2. Being a member of a democratic school has given me a greater sense of involvement in and responsibility for the school program.
3. Being a member of a democratic school allowed me to provide more individual attention to students and parents.
4. As a result of attending a democratic school, I get the impression that students develop a greater sense of involvement and responsibility for the school.

Responses to statement 1 ("Being a member of a democratic school has provided a more cohesive and integrated sense of purpose, goals, and measurements of success for our school.") were answered in the affirmative, ranging from yes, to definitely, to absolutely. The largest factor appears to be control of their situation:

"At my old school, I was very aware of being a cog. Although I enjoyed working with the kids, I knew that it was a dead-end job. This is so different now. I am in control of where we go and how we get there." Another similar comment: "I feel like I have an integral part in the decision-making process at the school. The responsibility is on me as well as my teammates to constantly address the needs of the school and how they directly relate to students. It is sometimes difficult to spread that expectation to everyone and urge them to voice it." And another practitioner said, "You create your own mission, so are not doing someone else's goals. You are allowed to do what you are passionate about."

These very positive comments were hedged somewhat by some other comments: "I believe the implementation of our sense of purpose and goals are becoming clearer, but success measurements need to be stronger and more tied to our mission. Our test scores are not good, but we have students, staff, and parents developing amazing self and human understanding and communication skills that will serve the future community they may live in. How is this measured?"

Indeed, how are the human skills gained by students measured? Or, how are democratic learning and leading skills measured? A fundamental problem in the democratic schools is that they need to lead to measurable standardized test scores immediately, or they do not appear to be making gains. Having only the standardized tests as the measure of school quality negates all the good that is done in creating democratic community; how involved students are in making choices and decisions, how involved the students and staff are in community, does not get measured by test scores.

Another hedge against the positive outcome of being in democratic control of their own schools is "again, teachers need extensive training/ preparation. Much is available, but it seems we need more." Indeed, past-driven isolation appears to be very difficult to eradicate.

However, comments such as these by the practitioners really solidify the previous comments about building community, consensus, the collective, the consultative, and the coaching commitment. Having the power to make the major decisions around the school mission empowers and makes goal setting more meaningful, and it makes building a common focus more a reality. It is not easy, but it appears to be worth the effort.

Responses to statement 2 ("Being a member of a democratic school has given me a greater sense of involvement in and responsibility for the school program.") were also positive. One practitioner commented, "Definitely true. I worked hard in the traditional system but was often undermined by decisions I had no voice in. Although it is a lot of work, I appreciate this aspect of our school a lot. We teachers take our job very seriously along with the responsibilities, no matter who is in charge and who is invited to participate." Another voice said, "When I see a problem here, I know that I must do more than gripe about it at the dinner table. I need to help fix it. I have done this by calling together focus groups, voicing concerns at meetings, and implementing changes."

And often that control and those changes lead to positive results for students: "Being led in decision making by a commitment to the students is a great benefit to the students," said one respondent. Another wrote, "I see the program tied closely with the purpose and goals of the school. We constantly address the needs in the program and who can step in and fill those needs." And another spoke of the responsibility: "You can't look toward someone else if things aren't getting done — you can't put the blame on someone else."

The greater sense of involvement leads to a greater ability to affect change for the benefit of the students. This is also a benefit to the educators, as they feel more empowered and energized by the power to affect what happens. Some teachers appear willing to accept that responsibility.

Responses to statement 3 ("Being a member of a democratic school allowed me to provide more individual attention to students and parents.") were in the affirmative for the most part. One wrote, "Even though I have worked in small programs in the past, I have never known students and families like I do now. The level of comfort and trust is fully refreshing." Another said, "We value working with a small group for the long term. Therefore, developing relationships with students and parents is a must. That allows me to address the students and family as a whole in developing their learning program." And another comment highlighted the difference between teaching in a traditional setting and a democratically controlled setting: "I used to see 160 students a day and 25 percent of the parents at conferences. Now I deal with 17 to 18 advisees and conference with all the parents once a month or more."

The only cautionary answer was "In many ways the opposite is true. With all the additional administrative duties and learning, planning for something with students to improve learning gets postponed to keep 'the school running.' There is potential staff to interview, reports to get in, and buildings to find and care for. I now understand how bureaucracies develop. I am hoping as we are more established, this will improve."

The ability to work with students and parents in a different ratio than in previous high school experiences appears to be a positive for the practitioners. Having small advisory groups and small school settings allows for the personalization necessary to really help students grow. A negative is, again, the time and skills necessary to do the job well.

Responses to statement 4 ("As a result of attending a democratic school, I get the impression that students develop a greater sense of involvement and responsibility for the school.") were also overwhelmingly positive, as attested to by the following:

"Definitely. Our Monday all-school meetings are student-run. The student congress identifies issues and brings them to the community. Also, our circle meeting (weekly) continues to be a place for students to air concerns and celebrate successes."

"Yes, because they see the teachers involved and asking for assistance (decision making as well as menial tasks) and therefore believe they have a say and can make a difference."

"Definitely. They claim their say in the program and expect to get responses to their requests. The constitution has been a remarkable way of showing that at our school." (The school has a constitution written by students.)

"I think students do have more involvement and say in our school; but due to the fact that some rules and boundaries are necessary when groups of people work together, students are sometimes still unhappy they can't call more of the shots."

"Definitely. Students volunteer for things, greet adults cheerfully, own their own learning, clean their own work space, and learn their own time management. The buy-in is terrific."

Having students take more involvement in their own education and having students develop the skills necessary to become life-long learners is the overall goal of EdVisions Schools. The development of greater involvement and responsibility in the overall school process is a means for accepting that responsibility for self and for the greater society. By the comments made by the practitioners, it appears that the students are becoming more responsible citizens by taking the responsibility of making decisions for the school and for themselves.

This is the hope of the democratic school. By giving students responsibility to choose the how, when, and what of their high school education, by giving them a voice in the overall management of their school, democratic principles are being learned. And teacher-advisers who take upon themselves the reins of school management and collaborative decision making allow for democratic principles to be lived out in an everyday process. Democratic learning and leading can happen in schools, and it apparently is a very good thing for both students and educators.

CHAPTER 7

Creating the Culture of Collaborative Governance

Teacher leadership provides an inevitable and continual occasion for teacher growth. The teacher who is always leading and learning will generate students who are capable of both leading and learning.

—Roland Barth

It says much about American culture when educators say they do not have the skills to interact in a democratic governance structure. We certainly appear to be far removed from de Tocqueville's America, where the town meeting, with every voice able to be heard, was the norm. The culture of schooling has taken a turn away from democratic governance, as outlined by Matthews (2002), Gatto (2003), and others. Yet, there are movements toward shared decision making (including site-based management, principal–teacher partnerships, leadership/learning councils, distributed leadership, outlined in chapter 1). Creating a collaborative culture, which allows for both the development of democratic governance by teacher-leaders and decision making in the learning program by students, is a difficult task. But the practitioners that spent two or more years working in schools where democratic learning and leading were taking place highlighted some very positive outcomes. The promises appear so rewarding as to compel educators to continue the quest.

Why is it difficult to create a collaborative culture? Many reasons, but at the heart of the challenge is the requirement of mutually interactive commitment. Teachers have to become leaders on behalf of democratic governance. Indeed, unless they do and are successful, students would not have the opportunity to accept decision making as part of learning.

To be sure, the obstacles are many. It takes more time: teachers have to work at governance. They have to build democracy seamlessly into their advising. They have to alter their learning relationships with their students. Above all, they have to practice what they preach. And, sadly, they have to shed the old top-down culture and its lack of the skills needed to interact democratically. But of all the obstacles to overcome, none is more formidable and basic as that of the culture of teacher isolation.

Consider all the degrees of separation. Grade levels stand apart. Subject matter specialists seldom talk to other subject matter specialists. Supervisors observe, evaluate, and communicate with each teacher. Class schedules are so tight that many teachers grab a quick snack at their desks and often never talk to another teacher for weeks. There may be lesson-planning time, but it is never flexible enough to permit collaborative planning of lessons even though the research clearly supports it. And there is hardly ever a group collaborative review of student work, although, once again, the research argues for it. Is it not odd that for a profession dedicated to communication, teachers are such silent Lone Rangers?

One of the critical ways of eliminating or reducing such isolation is governance empowerment. Learning councils, site-based management teams, distributed leadership, and the ultimate version, teacher leadership, compel interactive sharing. The EdVisions model breaks down isolation by the makeup of relationships between student and advisers, by makeup of facilities and by the makeup of the program as well as the management model. In the EdVisions Schools' model, parents sign off on student projects, student work is assessed by teams of teachers, and students give presentations of their work to real-world audiences (see Newell 2002a, 2002b). By virtue of these reforms, teacher-facilitators are naturally thrown into the maelstrom and have to function as collaborative leaders.

At first, those involved in helping create teacher-governed schools felt that there would be a natural ability to function democratically. Although many start-up groups were able to function well together, probably because their commitment and mission were strong, many others were not. Much of the problem came from the addition of staff after the creative energies were dissipated. Many had not functioned in an atmosphere other than isolation. As the practitioners noted in the surveys, many of their colleagues did not have the skills or the inclination to want to participate in a democratic, open management. They had to learn it on the job and get what they could from EdVisions technical assistants and/or consultants.

Another past-driven obstacle is that teachers are not taught to be reflective about the whole of the education enterprise. They know their subject matter, they know some pedagogy, they know their students, but they seldom look at the rest of the enterprise. They are not willing to bother themselves with the policy and financial aspects of schooling. Isn't that what principals and superintendents do? If teachers were interested, they became principals, superintendents, or union leaders. Teachers, to function well in democratic learning and leading, must take responsibility for finding the solutions in whole-school decision making. This requires interdependence and aggressiveness, usually only exhibited in classrooms or in departments.

In the past decades, education has become subject to the pressure of add-ons. Increasingly, curricula are required to bear the additive and redemptive dimensions of being research based, assessment driven, test prepped, accountability aligned, data tracked, and so forth. Technology also has had to follow the same path of integration. Its supplementary or occasional extensions or enhancements of learning now have to join the mainstream and become parts of daily and planned instruction. Finally, student behaviors, either modified or redirected, have become the focus of character education to minimize bullying, civic education to promote citizenship, and, most recently, an ethics curriculum created by Junior Achievement to advance ethical decision making.

There is no question that all of these would be valued additions to education. But implementation is another matter. All overload an already-crowded plate. Teachers would be pushed in many directions at the same time. The training required would probably consume at least half of every school day for one year. Then, too, externally imposed additions generally lack sticking power. Not internalized, they often exhibit a short shelf life. Finally, just when education is asked to be more proactive and creative, it is forced to be the passive receiver of external enlightenment.

Is there any other way? Can the various proposed external salvations imposed from without be accommodated and embraced from within? Indeed, it can be argued that every one of the external add-ons noted here has an internal secret sharer or partner residing in embryonic or potential form within education itself. In other words, the impetus may only require that pressure be transformed into opportunity, school improvement into school reform. How that would work and what it might produce can best be demonstrated by exploring the extent to which character, civic, and ethical education can be better accommodated if it were built into and made an integral part of traditional educational processes and structures.

Building character, civic responsibility, and ethical behavior is not solely or even primarily an object of study but of experience. All child rearing needs the double value of not only "Do what I say" but also "Do what I do." A key experience is the extent to which schooling and learning are democratized. Learning by imitative behavior is itself more powerful than abstract lessons and even imparts reinforcing specificity to such instruction. The key question, then, is what dimensions of schooling and learning have the potential and experiential capacity to build character, civic responsibility, and ethical behavior? The area that quickly comes to mind is classroom management.

How democratic is typical classroom management? Traditionally, classroom management is the way teachers control student behavior, accommodate the implementation of lesson plans, cover the curriculum, and manage testing and time on task. In other words, the traditional classroom is the agent of instructional control and planning. In all cases, the teacher is in charge and inhabits the center. Learning flow is essentially unidirectional. For student exchange to occur, a teacher's approval must be sought. The teacher may further maintain her centrality by becoming the sole or principal source of learning.

Does it work? It seemingly has, for many decades. So why not just continue or tweak the process? Because as a singular system, it does not seem to be able to deliver new kinds of skills required of students entering into a new kind of work world. It already shows signs of falling short of reaching the higher levels of knowledge suggested by No Child Left Behind and facilitating test scores that enable students to graduate from high school and to succeed in college. Moreover, as basically a solitary management system, it faces inwardly and appears resistant to a more interactive relationship with other professionals and with parents and the community. The reinforcing correlation between classroom management and the teacher culture of the Lone Ranger may be jeopardizing not only the optimum relationships between learning delivery and learning achievement but also the interpersonal relationships between teacher and student.

Above all, present classroom management fails the test of following a democratic model. It is hierarchical and aristocratic, singular in its power base, unsolicitous of the input of other teachers, students, and parents, and generally immune from grassroots review. Students know who are the good teachers and who are not; and although their views are virtually infallible, they are seldom sought, let alone factored into evaluation.

How, then, can classroom management be changed so that it can more successfully internalize all that education is now being asked to accomplish, on the one hand, and exhibit a more democratic process that builds character, civic responsibility, and ethical behavior, on the other? Minimally, that involves three tasks: altering the direction of learning flow and its environment, changing the learning role of students, and altering the role of teachers. As Deborah Meier (2003) puts it, "Students need to see an adult community that actively and zestfully participates in the oral and written exchange of ideas and the forms of decision making that democracy promotes" (16).

In EdVisions Schools, the project-based learning environment adheres to the principle that knowledge democratically comes from multiple sources. There are many teachers, not just one. Learning also comes from other students. Learning is motivated by the need and desire to know. Learning is both experiential and conceptual. And, learning is a process, not just a product.

Student roles also change dramatically. Students create their own learning space, even have their own work stations. Learning is a participatory process between learner and facilitator. There are no hitchhikers; no one gets a free ride. All have active rather than passive roles. Self-focused discovery and assessment is the rule. This involves collaborative learning, collaborative leading. It is borne of the idea that "none of us is as smart as all of us." Learning and behavioral goals are the same: independence and interdependence.

The role of the teacher also changes dramatically. Her positioning is not at the head but at the hub of various centers. The primary goal is busy-ness—the constant sound of interaction; silence is deadly. Coordination is the task, not control. The goal is becoming increasingly dispensable by helping the learners become more and more independent. The teacher-facilitator becomes self-reliant and self-defining: the question is, "What do we need to know, and what are our sources?" The rule is asking for and securing help and using each other as resources. High standards of academic performance are set by generating generous expectations of student ability and self-esteem. Teacher and student design rubrics for differentiation and self-assessment.

The learning community becomes an evolving community of learners. Their relationships to each other are those of fellow equals entitled to life, liberty, and the pursuit of happiness and excellence. Access is assured so that no child is ever deprived of equal opportunity. But achievement is a variable.

With such changes, student management becomes schoolwide empowerment. As such, learning and behavior share the same goals and mutually contribute to building character, shaping civic relationships as the collective responsibility of all involved, and developing ethical and caring social relationships. Such changes in the learning environment require equal or even greater change in teacher governance if the teacher in turn is to be free and empowered to make the environmental and role changes required of a more liberated school environment. Indeed, we believe that the latter may hasten and even drive the former.

What we have learned is that the changes leading to new learning environments and a democratic collaborative will not come to fruition simply by "willing" them to be. We may wish the future of leadership to be democratic teacher leadership, in that the movement is future driven. But the past has a way of lingering, of holding onto itself by means of tradition, of precedence, of what is comfortable and known. By taking the risk and accepting the reality of more work, present-day practitioners who are experiencing the realities are blazing new ground. But they need support.

One of the ways in which practitioners can be helped is by staff development around the development of what we call an "intentional collaborative culture" of teacher governance. The intentional culture needs nurturing by the creation, first, of learning circles (see *Learning Circles* by Collay et al. 1998). Learning circles are formed by the building of community and the collective. Creation of new school cultures requires a missionary zeal; groups have to have the same goals, purposes, and mission. Founders (generally educators, parents, and community leaders) have that zeal when a school is created.

But it is the new hires, or partners, coming into the enterprise after it is formed who prove problematic. New partners coming into the scheme need to be supported by the consultative and the coaching commitment. By having procedures in place that match experienced advisers with new advisers, some element of coaching can take place. One way of having the consultative in place is to devote one staff meeting per week to learning, book talks, sharing of practices tried during the week. This procedure adheres to two learning circle concepts found in Collay et al. (1998): constructing knowledge through personal experience and supporting learners in their reflective practices. The process of creating annual reports that sum up student learning, staff development activities, and the actions needed to make the school improve forces reflective practice.

When these activities are supported and documentation of reflections and actions take place, then the group is well on the way to creating action research and strategic planning. Data-driven decision making becomes a natural part of the functioning of the school. What will follow is the improvement of the democratic school culture, thereby creating the democratic capacity among staff, parents, and students. This is the crux of democratic learning and leading.

EdVisions has established the need to help with the development of the community by making it a priority in its summer institute for new grantees. The need for the building of the community and creating procedures to allow for the collaborative to take place is now stressed. For example, it has been determined that sites need to consider the governance structure called the "EdVisions Model Governance" (Thomas 2003). The processes used to make decisions will in all likelihood make or break the democratic collaborative efforts. It is with that in mind that EdVisions asks sites to adhere to the following guiding principles: democracy, equity, clarity of value and roles, comparable worth, quality, and competency.

A learning community led by teacher-leaders constantly links what is learned to the way it is learned. Collaboration rules all. Teachers meet and develop shared strategies. Students are asked to meet with each other for the same ends. Parents and board members are included at every opportunity. Broader issues of curricula directions, goals, and what determines student success and evaluation are joint governance occasions for all constituencies. The time it may take for comprehensive input is often extended by an agreement to proceed by consensus rather than by majority vote.

The school board in the democratic EdVisions sites ought to have central authority over all policy and operations, whether a teacher-majority board or otherwise; roles and responsibilities not delegated to committees are retained by the school board. Committees make recommendations to the board. Committees can be a combination of staff members (both certified and noncertified), board members, parents, students, and community members when called for by the bylaws. Students should also be represented by a student advisory body, meeting periodically with the board. Parents should also be represented by a parent advisory board, meeting periodically with the board.

Suggested committees include curriculum and standards; special education; finance; personnel; and operations, with subcommittees, such as transportation, building and grounds, food service, student records and reporting, and technology, as needed. On a small staff, many members will have to double up on committees, or all will have to deal with everything. It is in this vein that many of the practitioners said that they did not have enough time in a day to devote to the running of the school: they had to make *all* the decisions. The committees ought to include knowledgeable parents and community members to share the workload, especially when the staff is small. When a staff becomes larger, more of the workload can be taken up by the committees.

To share the workload with all the members and to ensure that no one small group can take control of the majority of the decisions, EdVisions created some recommended bylaws: each staff person shall serve on at least one but no more than two committees each year; each committee member shall rotate off a committee every two years; a person shall not serve as a committee chair for more than one successive year; a person may serve both on the board and a committee; a person may be a compensated employee (i.e., finance coordinator, administrative function) and a committee member; students on committees are optional; parents on committees are optional; community members on committees are optional; a majority of the personnel committee will be licensed (certified) staff.

In the case of contractual obligations with a teacher professional practice, the personnel committee will report and consult with the board of the professional practice before the school board; and the board will communicate professional personnel issues with the professional practice board before it goes to the management team of the school.

These committee bylaws and procedures are lessons learned, often the hard way. We now know that community, consensus, the collective, the consultative, and the coaching commitment are more likely to occur if effective democratic procedures are in place. To ask that a site management team of nine to fifteen staff members sit around the table and hash out all the pros and cons of a particular decision wastes time. Committees ought to bring recommendations to the site management team and to the board for action. When parents or students have concerns, there is a mechanism for addressing those concerns. When parents, students, and community members are part of the decision-making matrix, the learning community will be stronger.

All of this is perceived as part of a teaching load and the learning process, not as extra or separate committee work. The democratization of the process is the structure—*it is the school*. Teachers as leaders and learners, along with students and parents, collectively run and manage the entire school. All the while they are creating new learning environments that change their roles with students. And the students in this new learning environment become active citizens, participants in and leaders of their own education. "The habits of democracy do not develop naturally, any more than mathematical competence does. One learns best by immersion and apprenticeship," says Meier (2003:16).

Finally, we come to the largely unaddressed issue of time. The plate is full; facilitating, advising, guiding, teaching, managing, complying with mandates from the state, and collaboratively making decisions leave very little for leading full lives with family. There is never enough time. Time needs prioritizing; we cannot add hours to days. Priorities in teacher-governed sites must be the independence and interdependence of the persons in their charge: the students. By being democratic leaders and learners themselves, the teachers model that independence and interdependence—that becomes the priority. Other teacher behaviors, such as lesson planning, delivering rather than facilitating, and managing, take a back seat. Time that is saved from those activities is put into managing and modeling. Lambert (2003) notes that teachers in these new roles over a three-year period will have developed new constructivist routines. Teachers must rethink their past assumptions, beliefs, and experiences. By being reflective within a learning community of support, teachers will learn to depend on each other more, hand over more of the "work" of schooling to the students and find that the time spent was well worth their while.

As Lambert (2003) says, "Learning and leading cannot be separated: leading is a form of learning together. Instructional programs that evoke student voice, apply principles of constructivism, attend to intrinsic motivation, build resiliency, and engage students in democratic governance—all within a small context, whether natural or contrived—develop the leadership capacity of students" (64). By taking the time to establish a learning community culture, by giving the students choice and decision-making powers in the learning program, and by managing in a democratic manner, teacher's time usage is prioritized to the maximum.

By collaborating, by coaching and consulting, by utilizing a committee structure that allows for consensual decision making, a group of school leaders create a community where all participate, where all assume their responsibilities willingly, and where all know they are doing the maximum amount of good for all children in their care. One of the practitioners quoted in the last chapter said that "the program [is] tied closely with the purpose and goals of the school" and that the staff "constantly address the needs in the program and who can step in and fill those needs."

Perhaps, only with such a collaborative culture of governance is it possible to achieve that rare integration that has proven so elusive to all educational systems: the seamless integration of administration, instruction, and evaluation. In fact, one can go further and claim that given the current incredible demands being put on all teachers and all schools, perhaps the only, as well as the best, chance of accomplishing those tasks with integrity and intelligence may lie with structures and cultures that inherently seek the integration of all systems as the ultimate form of collaboration and democratization. What may be education's future is a system that is the least systemic. It will accommodate flow, not impasse; share, not hoard information; and build relationships and communities, not adversarial oppositions and gaps. And above all, it will love learning.

Practitioner Responses to the Five Aspects of Collaboration

Following are the answers found on the returned surveys of practitioners pertaining to the problems and promises of implementing the five facets of a collaborative culture:

The problems with coming to consensus:

- Time consumption—the stress of finding time to commit to committee work. There are too many meetings. (It is time-consuming.) (It takes time.)
- Staff may lack knowledge, experience, and information needed to make sound decisions.
- Coming to consensus after listening to all voices in the committee and full staff meetings is tiring and exhausting and can be frustrating.
- The division of staff on small issues/personal preferences can interfere with the communal purpose.
- Requires much time and effort to get all on the same page.
- An effective decision-making body requires skills and a high level of personal awareness that is not well-developed in most people (because of the organizational structure of most other institutions).
- It is a slow process—many staff would prefer the difficult decisions be left to someone else. There is still a degree of "passing the buck."
- It is messy.
- It is unclear exactly what decisions have been made.
- We need training/understanding on how to implement this process effectively.

- Decisions are sometimes made slowly.
- Having time on some of the major decisions.
- Decisions by consensus are messy. It takes everyone's time. It is easy to fall into a power structure and may have a tendency for people to align themselves with the power.
- We still have people who speak "more" and "louder" and that intimidate some from speaking out.
- It is like herding cats—so many ideas and thoughts are presented. Time does not allow for all the discussion needed.

The promises and positives in implementing consensus:

- Great to have my voice heard and to hear other voices.
- It empowers all to be involved, heard, and continue growth.
- Rules and decisions can be modified when the situation changes or shifts.
- We have some great brainstorming that evolves into great new ways of doing things.
- Involvement and awareness in all levels of management means educators, who have the students' well being in mind as a primary focus, make decisions with the students in mind.
- The work and collaboration of the staff serves as a role model to students of interpersonal interaction and communication.
- It is democracy in action. The civic action is easier to instill in students when they actually get to practice it. It is easier to teach because those who teach it also get to practice it as well.
- Reaching consensus means all voices are heard.
- Everyone backs the decision, since everyone was a part of making it.
- Everyone shoulders the positive or negative results.
- Everyone has the opportunity to have firsthand involvement in discussions leading to decisions.
- Everyone is a key stakeholder and we lose the perception of "us versus them."
- It forces people into professional decisions that otherwise are made by others.
- If people are comfortable saying what they mean, stakeholders have the opportunity to have a great deal of input.

The problems with building and maintaining the collective:

- The development of an inclusive community requires skills and a level of personal awareness that is not well-developed in most people.
- The division of staff over small issues/personal preferences can interfere with the communal purpose.
- It requires a great deal of time and effort to get all on the same page.
- Decisions morph and change with individual situations, causing confusion and or resentment.
- Manipulators and strong-armed "threateners" can undermine and frustrate the process.
- Making decisions when some of the members are not present.
- It can lead to divisions between staff with licenses and staff without licenses in decisions pertaining to licensure and professional issues.
- People regress to old habits or what is comfortable if there are not enough strong voices for moving forward.
- One vindictive and manipulative person could control others.

The promises and positives of the collective:

- The mission is revisited often and is the basis for most decisions.
- All must take responsibility for decision making and the consequences.
- All individuals must develop strength and skills to hold each other accountable. We can't play the blame game.
- Common vision is incredibly exciting! Students and parents see that vision and adopt it quickly because it is coming as one voice. Strong spirit!
- The table on which planning happens must remain small, thus forcing the community to remain small, making it easier to keep a collective focus.
- All have a voice, take part, and can have ownership.
- We always have a check-in with staff.
- Decisions are approached from many different angles.

- For certain personalities, it satisfies the need for involvement.
- It forces continued reflection on vision and mission that traditionally was easily lost in the shuffle.
- The collective group can keep one person from controlling and regressing.

The problems with implementing the consultative aspect of the culture are:

- The constant new learning can be overwhelming and exhausting.
- Sometimes, ignorance is bliss. Understanding the politics can be demoralizing
- It is tiring, messy, and can be painful.
- It, too, takes time.
- We don't have quick, easy access to coaches or mentors.
- It is difficult to judge what the needs are and when someone is ready for the "next step."
- Who has time? This area is vital, but we have not made the commitment on a staff level to do as much as we should to help new staff learn the basis of what we are all about.
- Difficult people (divas) who are comfortable in what they are doing think they have a right to do what they want.
- Confrontation with those who are not following through is more difficult with a group than it is with principal to teacher.

The promises or positives of implementing the consultative aspect of culture:

- It is refreshing and revitalizing. It is good to sit down with others and hear about what you are doing well. It is also great to be in an environment where real help is always available because everyone is in such close contact with each other.
- The role modeling of learning is much more effective than lecturing on how to learn.
- The mentality of life-long learning with reflective practice gives students and staff the skills and confidence to adapt to new situations and environments.

- Reflection allows for us to see serious areas for change.
- The constant new learning can be exciting and gives a much better understanding of all aspects of education and the education system. This allows me to be more effective and satisfied. There were a lot more frustrating unknowns when I was in the traditional school system.
- We are actively involved in the profession—personal growth is greater.
- We are all learning together.
- We learn time management.
- We see that we are always learning.
- A group as a whole generally brings people back to reality.
- It is easier to determine what is needed for staff development when teachers have personal professional development plans.

The problems with developing the coaching commitment:

- Evaluating and supporting each other requires openness to new learning and understanding. It is hard and can be painful.
- It requires care and a high level of interpersonal communication for consistent and constructive criticism.
- It doesn't work so well for people who believe they are perfect, are afraid of change or criticism, or are unable to comment on others.
- This has personally been my greatest frustration: you want to be able to welcome however inexperienced staff to the school, teaching them the process. But there are major demands to opening a school and the work has to be divided among the staff. The balance seems almost impossible.
- We all are learning together—no one is an expert.
- There is learning by osmosis in our paired staff structure, but a more formalized "indoctrination" would help.
- Teachers are often too nice to confront each other at the expense of the mission. Smallness of the environment means having to live with them every minute of the day, so the tendency is to not get at the deeper issues.
- A majority of the staff may never buy in to the great ideas of one of the staff.

The promises and positives of implementing the coaching commitment mentioned by the staff members:

- Looking honestly at self and others in job performance can lead to a deeper understanding and appreciation of self and others. The added feedback opens us to more of the unknown.
- We model growth for students.
- The ongoing movement toward self-actualization is real.
- We learn to stretch ourselves.
- We become more comfortable interacting with peers.
- Our paired staff structure helps establish some consistency.
- The whole staff can participate in workshops together—can easily determine who is buying in and who isn't. It is tougher for an individual to sabotage a professional development plan because it is easier to see.
- Small groups of teacher-leaders can act as cheerleaders for others— always able to see what each other are doing.

The problems with creating and sustaining a caring community:

- We sometimes get too focused on pressing issues and what needs to be improved and not on what has been accomplished. We don't celebrate accomplishments enough.
- It requires a deep involvement in the lives of those around us— must know them as people.
- It is difficult to know what is required for sustainability. How much should be learning? How much community? Which comes first?
- Parents are too satisfied. We don't see them as often as we would like. Volunteer hours have dropped off significantly (the school is in its second year).
- The reality of pulling together along the same path is more difficult than the idea. Whereas we may share the common vision and mission, we may not agree on the same path to actualize these.
- Most people involved are strong, passionate individuals; when significant differences of opinion arise, it can be very difficult to move ahead. Because passions are strong, emotions become strong. People in our schools will ideally have a good understand-

ing of their personal needs and styles and be willing to be open to examine their motives when they "dig in." Sometimes we need to dig in; sometimes we need to bury the sword.

- Some stakeholders have not been involved enough to feel passionate and empowered.
- People are not accustomed to being listened to, or being responsible for speaking well and ethically. We don't know how to do it. It is time-consuming. Working together is hard, and you don't always get what you want. Finding a group of people who posses the needed skills can be difficult.
- Deprogramming students from the old ways into community is difficult.
- It is sometime hard to cheer each other on as a staff. We're often seeing how far we have to go without seeing how far we have come.
- Having time with staff to connect and help students connect is difficult to come by.
- It is difficult to know how to set the tone for each year.
- It is difficult helping students and peers who start or join the group later become part of the community.
- I like the idea of going out together to socialize, but who has the time? We have cliques here, and that is due to breakdowns of communication.
- A traditional school staff can hide in their classrooms, but we (students and staff) are in the open, warts and all, for all to see and judge—we live in glass houses.
- It is hard for students and some parents who have had difficulties in school to believe in adults and schools as a community.
- Students are often uncomfortable with adults caring for them because they have not had that in the past.

The promises and positives exhibited in regard to community:

- Monday meetings have become a place to celebrate what students are accomplishing. Students listen and applaud.
- We like each other. We really do. It really is a nice place to spend my day.

- The students watch out for each other—they hug each other after breaks and weekends and are glad to be back in school.
- Our community gives a sense of belonging and support for the development of skills and abilities.
- A well-functioning community means most problems are talked out and dealt with before they give rise to gossip, infighting, long-term disputes, and so forth.
- The community develops important methods for relating to people and serves to benefit everyone. It gives space for further progress.
- The community continues to grow with more networking. People are hearing about us and they want to get involved.
- After working with a family for a couple of years, the relationship is incredibly strong and supportive.
- Students see themselves as valuable members of the community and that being a citizen is as much a responsibility as a right. Many are extremely involved in and out off the school. As they get older, their view of community expands.
- Utilizing the talents and ideas of everyone in the community has a tremendous potential for sharing strengths and to create new and better ways of working together.
- Ideally it excites all people involved and they contribute their strengths and share burdens.
- It does open the opportunity for new learning, which I have definitely experienced. It can be exciting but also overwhelming.
- Being able to deprogram students from old isolated ways is a positive, also.
- We can integrate school with the greater community—it is not school on an island.
- We can teach a real social curriculum.
- It has been good for students to interact more with each other—they become more proactive in difficulties, and they often take the lead in conversations.
- The traditional relationships are to a great extent broken—many relationships with staff to staff, staff to student, and student to student can and do become more personal than in a traditional school. We have the opportunity to be a major adult figure in many students' lives.

- Smallness allows for a much greater chance to do what is best for children.
- Advisers build great relationships. We celebrate and mourn together as a community.
- It is a safe environment for students. Every student knows there is an adult who cares for them.
- Presentations of projects to the community and community service make great common connections.
- Using community experts builds a positive community.
- When a child feels safe and cared for, their learning increases exponentially.

Practitioner Responses to the Four Statements

In addition to considering problems and promises of the five aspects of a collaborative culture, practitioners were also asked to respond to four statements pertaining to teachers managing their schools:

1. Being a member of a democratic school has provided a more cohesive and integrated sense of purpose, goals, and measurements of success for our school.
2. Being a member of a democratic school has given me a greater sense of involvement in and responsibility for the school program.
3. Being a member of a democratic school allowed me to provide more individual attention to students and parents.
4. As a result attending a democratic school, I get the impression that students develop a greater sense of involvement and responsibility for the school.

Responses to the **first statement** (Being a member of a democratic school has provided a more cohesive and integrated sense of purpose, goals, and measurements of success for our school.) include the following:

* Definitely. At my old school I was very aware of being a cog. Although I enjoyed working with the kids, I knew that it was a dead-end job. This is so different now. I am in control of where we go and how we get there.

- Yes, because we all have a stake and all have responsibility.
- I feel like I have an integral part in the decision-making process at the school. The responsibility is on me as well as my teammates to constantly address the needs of the school and how they directly relate to students. It is sometimes difficult to spread that expectation to everyone and urge them to voice it.
- I believe the implementation of our sense of purpose and goals is becoming clearer, but success measurements need to be stronger and more tied to our mission. Our test scores are not good but we have students, staff, and parents developing amazing self- and human understanding and communication skills that will serve the future community they may live in. How is this measured?
- True, but, again, teachers need extensive training/preparation. Much is available, but it seems we need more.
- We are more cohesive and integrated in our purpose and goals, and we are working toward measuring success.
- Absolutely. You create your own mission, so are not doing someone else's goals. You are allowed to do what you are passionate about.

Responses to the **second statement** (Being a member of a democratic school has given me a greater sense of involvement in and responsibility for the school program.) include these:

- When I see a problem here, I know that I must do more than gripe about it at the dinner table. I need to help fix it. I have done this by calling together focus groups, voicing concerns at meetings, and implementing changes.
- Yes, though that responsibility is heavy. Being led in decision making by a commitment to the students is a great benefit to the students.
- I see the program tied closely with the purpose and goals of the school. We constantly address the needs in the program and who can step in and fill those needs.
- Definitely true. I worked hard in the traditional system but was often undermined by decisions I had no voice in. Although it is a lot of work, I appreciate this aspect of our school a lot. We teachers take our job very seriously along with the responsibilities, no matter who is in charge and who is invited to participate. People will often fight against and challenge the "leaders." Some is healthy; some is not.

- True. As a founder of the school, I feel we had this from the get-go.
- You can't look toward someone else if things aren't getting done—you can't put the blame on someone else.
- This is true 24/7!

Responses to the **third statement** (Being a member of a democratic school allowed me to provide more individual attention to students and parents.):

- Even though I have worked in small programs in the past, I have never known students and families like I do now. The level of comfort and trust is fully refreshing.
- We value working with a small group for the long term. Therefore developing relationships with students and parents is a must. That allows me to address the students and family as a whole in developing their learning program.
- I can't pass off difficulties to someone else. I must address them and seek out support when I need it. Likewise, I must offer support to other staff in their work with students.
- In many ways the opposite is true. With all the additional administrative duties and learning, planning for something with students to improve learning gets postponed to keep "the school running." There is potential staff to interview, reports to get in, and buildings to find and care for. I now understand how bureaucracies develop. I am hoping as we are more established, this will improve.
- Yes—or at least a small school allows this.
- I am able to work with individual students, not classes.
- Absolutely. I used to see 160 students a day and 25 percent of the parents at conferences. Now I deal with 17 to 18 advisees and conference with all the parents once a month or more.

Responses to the **fourth statement** (As a result attending a democratic school, I get the impression that students develop a greater sense of involvement and responsibility for the school.):

- Definitely. Our Monday all-school meetings are student-run. The student congress identifies issues and brings them to the community.

Also, our circle meeting (weekly) continues to be a place for students to air concerns and celebrate successes.

- Yes, because they see the teachers involved and asking for assistance (decision making as well as menial tasks), and therefore believe they have a say and can make a difference.
- Definitely. They claim their say in the program and expect to get responses to their requests (demands). The constitution has been a remarkable way of showing that at our school. [The school has a constitution written by students with staff support.]
- I think students do have more involvement and say in our school; but due to the fact that some rules and boundaries are necessary when groups of people work together, students are sometimes still unhappy they can't call more of the shots.
- Yes, as long as the students have been sufficiently deprogrammed.
- It varies from student to student, but I believe we are headed in the right direction.
- Definitely. Students volunteer for things, greet adults cheerfully, own their own learning, clean their own work space, and learn their own time management. The buy-in is terrific.

References

WORKS CITED

Andrade, H. 1999. The effects of instructional rubrics on student writing. *Educational Leadership* 44.

Apple M., and J. Beane. 1995. *Democratic schools*. Portions available: www.ascd.org/readingroom/books/apple95.html. Accessed July 2003.

Boyte, H. 2000. *Professions in public crafts*. A working paper for the New Information Commons Conference, Wingspread, Wisc. Available: www.publicwork .org/pdf/workingpapers/public%crafts.pdf. Accessed November 2003.

Brown, R., and J. Cornwall. 2000. *The entrepreneurial educator*. Lanham, Md.: Scarecrow.

Charter Friends Network. 2001. *Charting a clear course*. Available: www.ncbdc.org. Accessed September 2003.

Christensen, C. 2000. *The innovator's dilemma: When new technologies cause great firms to fail*. Boston: Harvard Business School Press.

Collay, M., D. Dunlap, W. Enloe, and G. W. Gagnon. 1998. *Learning circles: Creating conditions for professional development*. Thousand Oaks, Calif.: Corwin.

Crawford, C., and R. Dougherty. 2001. Updraft, downdraft? *Education Week*, June 6.

Dirkswager, E., ed. 2002. *Teachers as owners*. Lanham, Md.: Scarecrow.

Dyer, K. 2001. The power of 360-degree feedback. *Educational Leadership* 58, no. 5.

Elmore, R. 1996. Successful educational practices. In *Rewards and reform: Creating educational incentives that work*, eds. S. H. Fuhrman and J. A. O'Day. San Francisco: Jossey-Bass.

Gatto, J. T. 2003. *The underground history of American education*. Oxford: Oxford Village.

Ginsberg, M., J. Johnson, and C. Moffett. 2001. *School support teams.* Alexandria, Va.: Association for Supervision and Curriculum Development.

Glickman, C. 2001. *Revolutionizing America's schools.* San Francisco: Jossey-Bass.

Greenleaf, R. 1984. *Servant leader.* Mahwah, N.J.: Paulist.

Handy, C. 1994. *The age of paradox.* Boston: Harvard Business School Press.

Hill, P., L. Pierce, and J. Guthrie. 1997. *Reinventing public education.* Chicago: University of Chicago Press.

Lambert, L. 2003. *Leadership capacity for lasting school improvement.* Alexandria, Va.: Association for Supervision and Curriculum Development.

Mansfield, H., and D. Winthrop. 2002. *Alexis de Tocqueville's democracy in America.* London: Folio Society.

Matthews, D. 1996. *Is there a public for public schools?* Dayton, Ohio: Kettering Foundation Press.

———. 2002. *Why public schools? Whose public schools?* Dayton, Ohio: Kettering Foundation Press.

Meier, D. 2003. What does it take to build a school for democracy? *Phi Delta Kappan* 85, no. 1.

Murphy, J., and D. Doyle. 2001. Redesigning operating environments. In *Education Commission of the States governance notes.* Denver: Education Commission of the States.

Newell, R. 2002a. A different look at accountability: The EdVisions approach. *Phi Delta Kappan* 84, no. 3.

———. 2002b. *Passion for learning: How a project-based system meets the needs of 21st-century students.* Lanham, Md.: Scarecrow.

Reason, P., and H. Bradbury. 2001. *Handbook of action research: Participative inquiry and practice.* London: Sage.

Robbins, P. 2001. *Peer coaching program.* Alexandria, Va.: Association for Supervision and Curriculum Development.

Sergiovanni, T. 1994. *Building community in schools.* San Francisco: Jossey-Bass.

Smylie, M. 2000. Teacher preparation in school decision-making. *Educational Policy* 12, no. 3.

Thomas, D. 1996. *Professional development checklist.* Henderson, Minn.: EdVisions Cooperative.

———. 2003. *The comprehensive guidebook.* Henderson, Minn.: EdVisions Cooperative.

U.S. Department of Education. 1993. *Honor what we know, listen to what we say.* Washington, D.C.: Author.

ADDITIONAL RESOURCES

Barth, R. 2001a. *Learning by heart*. San Francisco: Jossey-Bass.

———. 2001b. Teacher leader. *Phi Delta Kappan* 82, no. 4.

Black, S. 2000a. *Assessing student learning*. Arlington, Va.: Education Research Service.

———. 2000b. Find time to lead. *American School Board Journal* 187, no. 9.

Boyte, H. 1993. Reinventing citizenship. *Kettering Review*. Available: www.publicwork.org/pdf/workingpapers/reinventing%20citizenship.pef. Accessed November 2003.

Buchen, I. 1998. Business sees profits in education. *The Futurist* 33, no. 5.

———. 2000. Radical vision of education. *The Futurist* 34, no. 3.

———. 2001. Teacher leadership: Saving the ship of fools. *Education Week*, March 28.

Creating a collaborative learning community. 2001. Principal Series. Alexandria, Va.: Association for Supervision and Curriculum Development.

Cuban, L. 1990. Reforming again, again and again. *Educational Researcher* 19.

Dyer, K., and J. Carothers. 2001. *The intuitive principal.* Thousand Oaks, Calif.: Corwin.

Fink, E., and L. Resnick. 2001. Developing principals as instructional leaders. *Phi Delta Kappan* 82, no. 8.

Hurley, J. 2001. The principalship: Less may be more. *Education Week*, May 23.

Lambert, L. 2001. *Building leadership capacity in schools.* Alexandria, Va.: Association for Supervision and Curriculum Development.

Martin-Kneip, G. 2001. *Professional portfolios for education.* Alexandria, Va.: Association for Supervision and Curriculum Development.

McCann, B. 2001. Teacher leadership revisited. *Phi Delta Kappan* (February).

National Commission on Governing America's Schools. 1999. Denver: Education Commission of the States.

Neuman, M., and W. Simmons. 2000. Leadership for student learning. *Phi Delta Kappan* 82, no. 1.

Richardson, J. 2000. Focus principal development on student learning. *Results* (September).

Sagor, R. 2000. *Action research.* Alexandria, Va.: Association for Supervision and Curriculum Development.

Scaling up the Minnesota New Country School model: A guidebook. 2001. Henderson, Minn.: EdVisions Cooperative.

Sebring, P., and A. Bryk. 2000. School leadership and the bottom line in Chicago. *Phi Delta Kappan* 81, no. 6.

Starnes, B. 2000. On dark times, parallel universes, and déjà vu. *Phi Delta Kappan* 82, no. 2.

Terry, P. N.d. Empowering teachers as leaders. *National Forum Journals* 28.

Troen, V., and K. Boles. 1993. Teacher leadership. *Teacher Magazine* 16, no. 2.

Tyack, D., and L. Cuban. 1995. *Tinkering toward utopia.* Cambridge, Mass.: Harvard University Press.

Tyson, H. 1993. *Who will teach the children?* San Francisco: Jossey-Bass.

Wagner, T. 2001. Leadership for learning: An action theory of school change. *Phi Delta Kappan* 82, no. 5.

Wilson, M. 1993. The search for teacher leaders. *Educational Leadership* 12, no. 1.

Index

About the Authors

Ronald J. Newell spent twenty-seven years as a high school history teacher and coach, four years in teacher preparation programs at the university level, helped begin the Minnesota New Country School, and now works with the Gates-EdVisions Project replicating the project-based model. He is also the author of *Passion for Learning* (ScarecrowEducation, 2003). He can be reached at rnewell@hickorytech.net.

Irving H. Buchen has taught and served as an administrator at the California State University, University of Wisconsin, and Penn State University. He is currently a member of the doctoral business faculty of Capella University, a distance education institution. He is also an active management and education consultant, a senior research associate with Comwell, HR Partners, and EdVisons, and he is CEO of his own training and coaching company. An active researcher, Buchen has published over 150 articles and numerous books including *Parents' Guide to Student Success* (2004) and *The Future of the American School System* (2003), both by ScarecrowEducation. He can be reached at ibuchen@msn.com.